Liberation Ethics

LIBERATION
ETHICS

JOHN M. SWOMLEY, JR.

The Macmillan Company · New York, New York

Collier-Macmillan Limited · London

The Macmillan Company
866 Third Avenue, New York, N.Y. 10022
Collier-Macmillan Canada Ltd., Toronto, Ontario

Library of Congress Catalog Card Number: 72-80176

First Printing

Printed in the United States of America

To Joanna, John and Jean

Contents

Liberation Ethics

1

DEMAND FOR LIBERATION

THE DEMAND for liberation is heard on every continent today. Black Americans want to be free from the control of white people. Latin Americans want liberation from North American imperialism or from their own military governments. Eastern Europeans want to get rid of Russian domination. Poor people everywhere need freedom from hunger. Millions all over the world live under the shadow or actuality of war, including taxation and conscription by rival military elites.

Liberation ethics begins with this fact of desperate human need to be free from whatever it is that threatens or enslaves. Liberation ethics holds that the goal of history is the liberation of man. Yet liberation is an impossible goal so long as men seek freedom for their own group at the expense of others. The truth evident in the fact of thermonuclear weapons and in the growing worldwide air, land, and water pollution is that we are all under the ax. All of us are likely to be doomed or saved together.

On the other hand those worldwide threats originate in the same divisiveness, drives for power, and low estimate of the lives of others that are obvious in racism, poverty, and other forms of oppression. Liberation ethics also begins with these specific problems, because those most obviously oppressed and those who identify with them are always the key to social change. The drama of freedom is always connected with a specific people such as the Israelite slaves in Egypt, black Americans, Vietnamese peasants, or Bolivian miners.

Liberation ethics is a response both to human need and to the biblical emphasis on redemption. In fact, liberation is simply a currently more acceptable or modern term for redemption. Both words mean setting men free from whatever it is that enslaves them. Many people think of liberation as a secular term with chiefly political overtones and redemption as a distinctively religious or theological word. Redemption, however, was at one time a word with no more religious significance than the term *liberation* implies today. A slave who was redeemed was set free; he was no longer the property of his owner. He was set free because someone paid a price to redeem him.

Today few men are enslaved by another human being. They are robbed of a rightful freedom by massive systems or structures of society. Some of these systems such as war and racism have been in existence for centuries. These systems are not the creation of one man nor are they continued merely because they benefit a few people. They are suprapersonal because they have an existence and dynamic of their own. Everyone is born into one or more of these systems, as black children and white children in the United States are born into largely separate social structures. Some social structures are so much a part of the way of life of a particular society that people accept them without thinking about them. People then tend to fit into the system and to accept the myths which support or rationalize it.

Many of these systems, such as the military or war system, are seen as necessary even by those who suffer the most from them. These people, therefore, have tended to think of individuals or groups who *administer* the system as their oppressors rather than the system itself. Again and again during the nineteenth and twentieth centuries men have tried to overthrow their oppressors, believing that this would end oppression. They have sought a more humane existence at an enormous human cost and yet their efforts at revolutionary social change have not achieved significant freedom for them or their children.

Liberation ethics is primarily social ethics because it holds that the elimination or the conversion of oppressors as individuals does not deal with the structures of oppression embodied in long accepted and interrelated social systems. The struggle for liberation is not a clandestine operation designed to destroy a few oppressors; it begins with an analysis of society different from one which sees some people as "good guys" who are to be liberated and others as "bad guys" who are to be subjugated or destroyed. The identification of persons as good or bad in this analysis is determined by their relation to the system. A young conscript is likely to have a different image of the draft board that conscripts him and of the subordinate officers who force him into the army mold than does a general. To the conscript they are likely to be the enemies of freedom; to the general they are necessary parts of a system he approves. Any system may be administered by tyrants or task masters, but it is the system which makes possible the tyranny rather than "bad" men who seek power over others and "good" men who seek to replace them.

All people are involved in evil, by which is meant anything that keeps men from becoming genuinely free, whether that thing is a social structure, an inner drive to attain authority over others, or some addictive personal habit. Everyone is to some degree corrupted by sin, which is the acceptance or willing of such unfreedom. Liberation ethics does not accent the transformation of systems on the ground that new men free from sin will emerge. That is a

Marxist error which asserts that a particular organization of society will make perfect human beings. However, the way society is organized does condition human conduct. And humans can be improved by membership in a community that respects each person as a brother or sister.

A concentration on changing systems does not mean that persons are less important. They are so important that they must not be used as tools of any system. The idea of liberation or redemption therefore includes love because it indicates that the persons to be set free have worth or dignity. No one thinks of freeing a tool or an inanimate object, for it is useful only insofar as it is possessed and used. A person is more valuable because he is capable of community, of loving and being loved.

The original use of the word *freedom* throws light on its meaning for ethics. In old English the word *free* meant "dear" or "loved" as it applied to the non-slave and non-animal members of a household. It came from the word *freon* (to love). The word *friend* comes from the same root. There is in this concept of freedom the idea of rights belonging to human beings who are dear or loved because they are not considered as tools. Anyone whom we genuinely love or whose person we respect must be free to realize his selfhood or to pursue his potentiality to the fullest. Love is the affirmation rather than the possession of another.

Freedom really means belonging to the beloved community. In ancient Greece freedom was associated with citizenship in the community or city-state. Slaves and barbarians were human beings but not held in the same esteem as citizens. In the United States the lack of freedom which minority groups experience in spite of their citizenship is derived from the fact that many whites are unable to think of blacks or Indians or Chicanos as actual or potential friends. They are to all practical purposes considered outside of the community. The purpose of liberation ethics is to include everyone in the beloved community so that there are no slaves or second-class citizens. In the case of these minorities this does not mean integration into a white world and its value system but into a community where black values and experience as well as those of other groups play an important role.

The goal of liberation ethics is community rather than any particular political or economic system. By community is meant a unity of persons around the idea that each is important enough to be respected and loved by all. It means that I want every other person to be as free and as loved as I want to be. Liberation, then, implies a quality of life that asserts the importance and worth of persons in such a way that they are free from poverty, from control by more powerful interests, from superstition, fear, hostility, or from anything that enslaves them.

The use of the word *community* does not imply only a quality of life but also a structure in which production is subordinated to the needs of persons. The reason we do not speak at the outset of some specific political or economic system as characteristic of a liberated society is partly that no currently operating system embodies liberation. It is also true that no whole system can be presented in advance of the struggles and problems of liberation. The goal of liberation then is to be found not in a blueprint but in a general direction which dynamically meets the real needs of persons. That general direction is summarized in the idea that men and women are not a means to be used for profit or for war or nationalism or racism or anything else that denies their full humanity. They are intended to live in community without structured exploitation or segregation.

Such community is not exclusive or parochial in the sense of nation, race, or intimate association. It is the belonging to every other being because he or she is human and therefore deserves our respect and concern. Yet we are also born into or acquire national, racial, political, economic, or the other loyalties that are divisive. It is the yielding to these lesser loyalties and to the lack of trust in the larger community as the purpose and goal of human existence that is the root of man's most savage or cruel behavior. People who are reasonable and decent within their own group will kill, torture, degrade, or otherwise treat enemies of their group as less than human.

Although liberation involves the greatest possible respect for and affirmation of our fellow humans, there is in each of us some will to insure our own security and even primacy which is the root of unfreedom. This will to survive and to be accepted which is apparently present at birth is not in itself evil but is the root both of freedom and unfreedom. Security and acceptance, in the full meaning of these words, are possible only in the most complete human community. Yet they are most likely to be identified with the more parochial groups to which we have become accustomed. A black man is really secure and accepted only when there is no white racist threat to his survival and no social structure from which he is excluded because of his blackness. Yet most white and black persons in the United States apparently feel more secure and accepted in the familiar racial groups in which they have been reared even though such division creates its own insecurity.

It is the intense loyalty to, or deification of, the nation-state, the economic, political, racial, military, or other structures which men have viewed as necessary to their survival or acceptance that makes the elimination or transformation of those structures so difficult. Yet the fact of exclusion of other groups from a more adequate and social existence also serves to increase their demand for systemic or structural change. Man, in other words, is neither doomed by his nature to a narrow loyalty nor assured of maturing into a full human community; but he is equipped with the need to love and be loved, with the desire to be free and to set free, and with a common humanity that makes him interested in and curious about other persons. It is when he becomes thoroughly committed to liberation, to the purpose and goal of human community that he is saved from his lesser loyalties and from the dehumanizing impact of the structures designed to serve those loyalties.

The act of commitment is not caused by the process of intellectual consideration of the value of liberation but by one or more events that compel him. These events may be the experience of oppression, or outrage at another person's hurt, or being treated as fully human at an undeserving moment, or becoming a part of a group that is integrated on a higher level than he is. Events, however, necessarily involve reflection or some weighing of their meaning before commitment to liberation becomes a part of anyone's total way of life. Liberation, in other words, involves not simply a desire to be free or to set someone free but also a conviction that it is of the essence of morality.

The moral foundation of liberty is not, as John Stuart Mill put it in his essay "On Liberty," in utility or in its contribution to the happiness of the greatest number of people, but in the fact that it is intrinsically right. No human being can be himself or give of himself under external compulsion so well as he does freely. Those who live under any form of oppression even in a nominally free society develop the mind and mood either of the slave or of the rebel. The slave does what is required of him unwillingly. Because he works slowly, he may appear to be lazy; because he dare not be caught in a deliberate slow-down, he may appear stupid by "understanding" only the immediately clear orders; because he is depressed by his lack of self-respect stemming from a lack of respect by others, he may develop a reputation for being dirty or for not caring about neatness and certain other personal and property values important to his "superiors." Those who manifest none of these more extreme characteristics simply conform to what is expected in order to avoid the consequences of defying the system. The mind of the rebel is one of resentment. He has a tendency to engage not only in slow-downs but in sabotage by putting sand in the machinery. He appears sullen or resentful and given to expressions of hostility which put others on guard. He creates fear, hostility, and watchfulness or suspicion on the part of those who support or administer the system.

There is of course no such thing as the complete absence of compulsion, because every society is governed by some rules or laws. But there is a difference between laws or restrictions which people approve as helpful to achieving their goals and those which they see as intended to serve others at their expense.

The emergence of democracy, or government by elected representatives, at a time when people were ruled by kings or feudal hierarchies theoretically made the people sovereign. But those who resisted rule by kings were those who had already achieved some status or property; they were not the poorest of the king's subjects. Their laws written in parliaments, diets, or congresses operated in the interests of people like themselves whom they represented and understood. Consequently they felt they had achieved freedom. They substituted rule by their class of people for rule by the king. The poor and dissenting groups who felt excluded or unaccepted had yet to experience freedom.

Freedom must always be discussed in context, since it is impossible to be free from all conditioning influences. It is normally defined by the absence of some compulsion, restraint, or impediment which keeps people bound to their own or others' habits or interests. True liberty, however, is found not only by those who are no longer bound by such imposed interests, but also by those who seek this freedom for all men. Immanuel Kant properly suggested that the right to be recognized as a free man carried with it the imperative of treating others not as means to an end but as ends in themslves. There is also a necessary relationship between freedom of the individual person and a free society. Where there is no genuine freedom for individuals it can hardly be said that the society or group of which they are a part is a free society. But there is also a liberty that belongs to social groups so that they are protected against the self-seeking of egoists, individualists, and corporations and against the messianism of would-be dictators.

Liberation then requires both freedom for the individual and a free society. Society, however, never becomes and stays free. There are always "good" practices or structures that become institutionalized and hence become repressive. For example, the idea that no one's freedom should be infringed unless there were a clear and present danger to others, was intended to broaden rather than restrict freedom. But insofar as governments and nation-states can allege a clear and present danger it puts them in a privileged position because in political crises any freedom can be qualified or set aside. Thus an entire racial or other minority such as Americans of Japanese descent during World War II could be placed in concentration camps because governmental authority saw their freedom as a clear and present danger. Since freedom is always dynamic in the sense that it is a perpetual process, liberation also includes continuing participation in the freeing of those who become victims of any institution or practice.

No one can participate in the process of liberation without realizing its cost. To oppose the existence of the military establishment or racial segregation in a society that views its survival and security as involved in these structures is to run some risks. Setting men free from any powerful interest is costly. Liberation, unlike the original meaning of the word *redemption*, does not imply the paying of a ransom such as wealthy parents do for a kidnapped child. Liberation is costly because the powers that enslave are so strong that it is necessary to pay a price to oppose them. Those who plan for revolution or who in some societies simply engage in dissent, know that it can be done only at the risk of status, reputation, property, and life.

Many who work for liberation, while prepared to run personal risks, think of making their adversaries pay the greatest price. This is the approach of revolutionaries such as Robespierre, Lenin, Mao Tse-tung, Castro and counterrevolutionaries such as Napoleon, Franco, and Stalin.

This assumption that we shall make others pay is a by-product of three obsolete ideas. The first is that those who have oppressed us should in some way receive a dose of their own medicine or experience the pain they have inflicted on us. This is revenge. The second is that it is possible for one group to be liberated by a process that enslaves or degrades others. This is a throwback to individualism, to the idea that personal profit or advancement can occur only if some other person experiences loss. Both of these ideas depend on a false analysis of the root of unfreedom. That false analysis is based on the assumption that oppression is caused by evil individuals or groups; that if they can be defeated or eliminated or forced to change places with the oppressed, liberation will have taken place. The third obsolete idea is that those in power determine by their resistance to change whether and how much violence there will be. This idea falsely holds that violence must always be met with violence or that the dispossessed fight better when they choose the methods or weapons of the oppressor. When put simplistically it is said that one must fight fire with fire. But sometimes it is better to smother a fire by depriving it of oxygen or to pour water on it or to isolate it. There are, in other words, a number of ways by which change takes place so that the oppressor is not inevitably able to determine the methods of liberation. There are nonviolent methods of resistance such as withdrawal of economic support via boycott or strike. These methods of course depend on numbers of people rather than on fire-power of weapons. Hannah Arendt makes a distinction "between power and violence," asserting "that power always stands in need of numbers, whereas violence up to a point can manage without them because it relies on implements."[1] This suggests that the larger the numbers de-

---

1. Hannah Arendt, *On Violence* (New York: Harcourt, Brace & World, Inc., 1969), pp. 41, 42.

manding change, the less is their need to rely on violence. But it also implies that minority reliance on violence can be nullified by superior technology. It is a mistake for the oppressed to let their oppressors choose the weapons they can use more effectively.

Another approach to liberation is that of the just revolution modeled after the medieval Christian concept of a just war. A just, violent revolution is waged only when (1) there is gross injustice on the part of the ruling class, (2) all nonviolent means to eliminate the injustice have failed, (3) there is moral certainty that the side of justice will win, and (4) there is a clear intention to bring into being a just order rather than a mere shift of the reins of power. A just revolution must also be (1) rightly conducted: restrained within the limits of justice and love, (2) fought so that guilt and punishment must be proportionate. Punishment exceeding the measure of guilt is unjust and therefore prohibited, and (3) careful to avoid unnecessary destruction of lives and property not immediately endangering the revolution.

It would be difficult for anyone who believes in radical social change to indict those who engage in violent revolution if there is great injustice and if repeated efforts to eliminate it by organized nonviolent direct action have failed. Unfortunately the various modern revolutions such as the Russian, Chinese, Algerian, Spanish, and Cuban were not begun after nonviolent methods failed, but were started because of initial assumptions that violent methods were essential to revolution. In evaluating future revolutionary efforts there should be some criteria for the success and failure of nonviolent actions. Nonviolent struggle, such as strikes, boycotts, and sit-ins, can be said to be successful if they accomplish a limited purpose and if that achievement results in some transfer of power or in partial democratization so that new demands can be made from a position of greater strength. They can be said to have failed if there is a revolutionary situation but aggressive nonviolent struggle is again and again defeated. The reason for speaking of a revolutionary situation is that neither violence nor nonviolence can succeed if there is no social basis to support revolution.

The question whether violent revolution can be won depends upon the context. In an unindustrialized country against a largely unindustrialized foe the chances of winning are greater than in a society where an efficient ruling elite has all the advantages of modern technology. These advantages lie not only in destructive weapons but also in electronic and other methods of detection. Given the technical development of the implements of violence there can be no reasonable certainty that the side of justice will win. If, nevertheless, a revolutionary group should begin armed conflict against superior numbers and superior technology there is no reason to assume that it can or will use violence with restraint. The escalation of violence by the ruling elite is likely to result in further escalation by the revolutionists.

Still another approach to liberation rejects armed violence for perhaps different reasons. One reason is that a just revolution is to all practical purposes impossible given the development of state power and weapons technology in the hands of large nations such as the United States and the Soviet Union. Another reason is the belief or conviction that there is no single road to liberation, that nonviolent methods are always possible. A third reason is that human solidarity and the worth of persons are more important than anything else; that oppression is primarily rooted in systems rather than in persons or groups of persons who profit from them; and that armed violence presupposes the destroying or subjecting of one group by another. It is obvious that the use of armed violence is intended to use whatever means are necessary in order to take power from the ruling class and hold it at their expense. But the phrase "ruling class" always includes the armed soldiers, police, and other supporters of that class who are poor or in lower income brackets. It is these who suffer most directly in loss of life or through injury. There are also others who are not friendly to disruption of law and order or who abhor armed violence. These too suffer.

The approach of liberators such as Jesus, Gandhi, and Martin Luther King assumes that participation in the struggle for liberation requires the paying of a price rather than exacting it from others. Liberation of your enemy is an integral part of achieving freedom for yourself because it is the system that enslaves both. If an enemy is subjugated and the process of superiority and inferiority continues, oppression is not ended.

In summarizing these various approaches to liberation it is essential to note that there are no guarantees of success simply from choosing one over others. The function of liberation ethics is to provide guidelines for action that will humanize rather than brutalize persons, that will help solve problems rather than proliferate them, and that will be useful in evaluating the methods and consequences of social change. There are always moral as well as pragmatic dilemmas in choosing a course of action that may lead to loss of lives, or to failure, or to immediate success but ultimate failure.

Liberation ethics is concerned not only with the goal of freedom but with the process of setting men free. The process or method of liberation is in turn determined by motivation. An effort to seek freedom for oneself alone results in action quite different from that of the intentional liberation of others. Similarly, a desire to liberate enemies as well as friends will result in methods different from those used in trying to liberate friends by destroying enemies. The question of attitudes toward any group of adversaries is in turn determined by political or social analysis. If it is the political and economic structures that permit some men to have unusual power and cause others to have little, then basic structural change is required.

Any structure that involves the centralization rather than the decentralization of power deprives the majority of people of the determination of their own destiny. Governmental structures put the war-making decisions in the hands of a relatively small group of persons whose interests are determined by their position in military, financial, and political systems. Decisions about conscription, taxation, public health, welfare, and the regulation of monopolies are made by a few hundred elected and appointed officials and the systemic interests which influence them. Similarly policies relating to production, prices, profits, and overseas investments are determined by a relatively small group of business and financial leaders.

The goal of liberation therefore includes the decentralization of decision-making power or the transferring of power to the people. Real revolution does not involve the transfer of power from existing power structures to a new power elite but to the people so that they determine their own destiny. Traditional revolutionary thinking looks to the seizure of power at the top. Liberation, however, may require a strategy of progressive conquest of power in local branches of industry, local communities, and educational institutions. Such progressive conquest need not be reformist or designed to improve existing systems. It can and should be revolutionary in that each struggle moves in the direction of a radical transformation of society giving more and more power to the people. Liberation, then, is progressively realized rather than postponed until some postrevolutionary period; yet the emphasis is not on gradualism but on strategies that are effective short of an all-or-nothing approach characterized by most revolutionary doctrine.

Another fundamental difference between liberation ethics and a traditional revolutionary approach is in the treatment of persons during and following the conquest of power. Regis Debray summarized this position in a statement made in November 1967, in Bolivia after his trial for being a member of Che Guevara's guerrilla band:

Naturally the tragedy is that we do not kill objects, numbers, abstract or interchangeable instruments, but, precisely, on both sides, irreplaceable individuals, essentially innocent, unique for those who have loved, bred, esteemed them. This is the tragedy of history, of any history, of any revolution. It is not individuals that are placed face to face in these battles, but class interests and ideas; but those who fall in them, those who die, are persons, are men. We cannot avoid this contradiction, escape from this pain.

Liberation ethics holds that it is possible to avoid this contradiction, that it is possible to battle systems, interests and ideas without killing or injuring persons. It is not necessary to seize power in an armed confrontation; it is only necessary to withdraw power from those who administer the system by refusing to cooperate with them. However, it is also possible to take power. As Martin Luther King put it:

There is more power in socially organized masses on the march than there is in guns in the hands of a few desperate men. Our enemies would prefer to deal with a small armed group rather than with a huge, unarmed but resolute mass of people. . . . All history teaches us that like a turbulent ocean beating great cliffs into fragments of rocks, the determined movement of people incessantly demanding their rights always disintegrates the old order. It is this form of struggle—non-cooperation with evil through mass actions—"never letting them rest"—which offers the more effective road.[2]

Liberation ethics is also concerned about the consequences of any form of action designed to set men free. An analysis of the consequences of the major revolutions of our modern world is therefore essential since these revolutions have helped shape the thinking of millions of people. The primary question in any analysis of the results of revolution is whether they have been genuinely liberating. A

2. Martin Luther King, Jr., "Never Let Them Rest," *Liberation*, April 1968, p. 12.

revolution can be said to have failed if little has been accomplished in return for all the lives lost and the hardships endured, or if in fact one dictatorship has supplanted another or one imperialism replaced another. It is more than of passing interest that many who seek revolution, including a socialist philosopher such as Herbert Marcuse, should indicate that the major socialist societies of our day, all of which have been built by armed revolution, have already succumbed "to repressive forces within their own system." Marcuse goes on to say that "unless socialism is built by such a new type of human being, the transition from capitalism to socialism would mean only replacing one form of domination by another form of domination . . ."[3]

This statement goes to the heart of ethics. Can a liberating social structure be built by those who do not in themselves represent the essence of the new society? Can a society intended to respect everyone after the revolution be built by those committed to destroying their enemies during the revolution? Such questions are not intended as an indictment of revolution, but to set the stage for exploring alternate methods of social change. At this point in history the need for transforming systems is so great that "revolutionary" may be the only term that can be used for the changes that must come. Certainly the demand for liberation becomes more urgent with every passing day.

3. Herbert Marcuse, "Marxism and the New Humanity: An Unfinished Revolution," in *Marxism and Radical Religion: Essays toward a Revolutionary Humanism*, John C. Raines and Thomas Dean, eds. (Philadelphia: Temple University Press, 1970), pp. 4, 7.

2

LIBERATION ETHICS: A CONTRAST

Lー IBERATION ETHICS may be understood more clearly in contrast to certain other ethics. It differs, for example, from "love-your-neighbor" ethics in that it takes far more seriously the need for transformation of social structures. It differs also in that it places a greater emphasis on concern for enemies. Both of these differences are made dramatically clear in any analysis of the war system.

During World War II, war was evil but acceptable to most "love-your-neighbor" ethicists. It was permissible to kill those on the other side because the war system was not the enemy; it was opposing nations and their inhabitants who were enemies. Many of those who lived within the borders of enemy nations were acceptable targets because it was necessary to destroy their war industry, and few population centers could be said to be unrelated to the war. The emphasis on love under such circumstances was practically reduced to exhortations not to hate. Professor Edward LeRoy Long, Jr., described the ethically concerned Christian as an "agonized participant" who believed war

should be "kept free of vindictive hatred for the enemy."[1]
War was regarded as the lesser evil in a choice limited to
war and only one other alternative: submission to the
enemy. Other choices were excluded by design so as to
predispose a choice of war.[2]

Liberation ethics, on the other hand, is primarily concerned with eliminating or transforming systems. War is
the enemy, not the young men on either side who were
conscripted to fight each other. Liberation ethics does not
view war or any other system of one's nation, race, or
social group as a lesser evil to be accepted while human
beings who are loved in the abstract are killed or segregated or exploited.

For most people the "enemy" in wartime is a political
unit and its people, such as the Germans or the Russians.
Such "different" groups with apparently different interests
also exist within nations. Many Americans regard blacks,
Jews, Chicanos, Indians, or political partisans of the extreme Right or Left as not belonging to the community.
The enmity of many Americans to these minority groups is
evident in the various systems that hold minorities down.
These systems include the Indian reservation, the black
ghetto, anti-Semitism, and the imprisonment of Communists for party leadership or membership rather than for
overt criminal acts. Some of these Americans who have
been taught love of neighbors are "agonized participants"
in these systems and make an effort at non-hatred or even
friendliness toward the individual black man or Jew or
Indian. Yet they also support the local and national social
structures that perpetuate the discrimination.

Liberation ethics accents freedom more than it does love
because any love of the oppressed which does not result in

1. Edward LeRoy Long, Jr., *War and Conscience in America*
(Philadelphia: Westminster Press, 1968), p. 44.

2. See the author's discussion of the lesser evil in *American
Empire* (New York: Macmillan, 1970), pp. 31–33.

efforts to achieve their liberation is hypocrisy. It accents freedom because only free persons can participate genuinely in community. Liberation, however, is not the negation of love, because any ethics concerned with freeing persons from oppressive systems must be guided by love for those trapped in them.

Liberation ethics also differs from those approaches to ethics that emphasize justice. Reinhold Niebuhr, for example, while maintaining the norm of love, insisted that in political and economic relations the primary emphasis should be placed on justice.

Niebuhr moved in his thinking from a primary concern for the problems of the dispossessed and the workers who needed social change to the maintenance of a democratic tradition in which the power of labor and ethnic minorities is to some degree balanced against the greater power of the upper classes. He criticized and condemned the capitalist system while supporting a mixed economy in which capitalism would have the major role. Emil Brunner who also emphasized justice wrote: "We can speak of a just law or system, but we cannot speak of a loving law or system."[3] Justice is always relative. Brunner indicated that anyone regarded from the standpoint of justice is viewed as "fitting his place in the structure, as one whose place has been decided upon, and so decided that this or that is his due or property." His due are his rights within "the whole structure."[4]

Liberation ethics differs from those emphases on justice which seek to give the poor and minorities a modest stake in existing political and economic systems, or which seek to make oppressive institutions such as war tolerable by arms control or just war rules. Justice is really a by-prod-

3. Emil Brunner, *Justice and the Social Order* (New York: Harper and Brothers, 1945), p. 16.
4. Ibid., p. 19.

uct of freedom. Probably the best short definition of injustice is *that which dehumanizes man.* So justice is that which is a man's due—his birthright as a human being, or human dignity. This means that each person must be free from poverty, from authoritarian rule, from racial discrimination, from conscription, war, and many other systems that keep him from being his best self. Justice demands these things; liberation is the process of seeing that they are achieved.

Liberation ethics may also be understood more clearly in contrast to a rules ethics and the currently popular situation ethics. The use of rules as a guide to human conduct is at least as old as the Ten Commandments (Exod. 20:3–17). It is as modern as the laws which are drafted in each legislature to regulate human relations. A rules ethics is based on the similarity of many situations, so that it is possible to generalize about what people should or should not do in comparable situations. It is also possible to think of exceptions to rules. For example, a starving man lost in the mountains would be justified in stealing food from an unoccupied forest ranger station. But the occasions when stealing could be justified are less numerous than those in which another person's possessions should be respected. Other rules deal with situations where it would be difficult or impossible to imagine valid exceptions. Forcible rape, for example, is wrong because it always involves a lack of respect for women. A rules ethics is derived from generalizations about human conduct that are intended to encourage respect for persons. Respect for others, according to those who hold to rules ethics, is learned and transmitted throughout history not only by emphasis on love of neighbor but also by specific rules that embody that love in concrete situations.

Liberation ethics, however, does not rely on rules. It emphasizes a life style or orientation of respect for persons. The rule is less important than the purpose of serving human need which presumably gave rise to "good" rules in the first place. Some rules and many laws are integral to the systems or structures which do violence to persons, and should be disobeyed. A law requiring military training or other forms of "service" to the state is unjustified and therefore should be resisted. The primary question is whether the state exists to serve its members or whether it is the state that should be served. Resistance to unjust laws is older than English and American rejection of the edicts of tyrannical kings. There are incidents of such resistance in biblical and other ancient writings.

Liberation ethics advocates both civil disobedience to laws which humiliate, demean, or exploit persons, and also refusal to accept rules which have the same effect. It is much more concerned with changing systems than in sustaining the rules of outmoded structures, although it recognizes the validity of rules and laws which are intended to enhance respect for human life, and seeks to strengthen them.

Situation ethics differs from rules ethics in beginning with the assumption that each situation is unique and therefore requires a different application of love or respect for persons. It asserts that there are no rules. Love is to be used as a norm for conduct at each point of moral choice so that the validity of any action including stealing or murder is determined by the situation plus love. Joseph Fletcher, the foremost American exponent of situation ethics, has abstracted the principle of love from the New Testament and asserted that "whatever is the most loving thing in the situation is the right and good thing." This implies that an ethical action is determined chiefly by love as motivation. But the illustrations or case studies used in books on situation ethics often reveal a very parochial concept of love, such as love of party or love of country. A Viet Cong terrorist, for example, who gives his life while carrying a hidden bomb into a Saigon officer's club is described as an example of "selfless, calculating concern for others" even though there may be a question "whether correctly (perhaps fanatically) decided or not."[5] There is no analysis of the consequences or probable consequences of terrorism, or whether the killing of enemies actually contributes to a concern for others or whether killing as a method dehumanizes on such a scale as to cast doubt upon it.

In one of Fletcher's illustrations of situation ethics, there is an attractive twenty-eight-year-old Christian woman who has been asked by the United States military intelligence agency to seduce for blackmail purposes a married man who worked for a rival nation in a city in Western Europe. Fletcher indicates that he discussed this with the young woman "as a question of patriotic prostitution and personal integrity. In this case, how was she to balance loyalty and gratitude as an American citizen over against her ideal of sexual integrity,"[6] This illustration could be analyzed as a struggle between the woman's traditional religious training against adultery, and patriotism, which is the way it is presented in *Situation Ethics*. The same illustration, if analyzed from the standpoint of liberation ethics, would be used to raise questions about the structures of nationalism, militarism, and espionage. Does a Christian or anyone else concerned about human beings owe primary allegiance to such structures of violence or is there a larger loyalty? Is patriotism or citizenship to be identified with the worst features of national life or can "loyalty and gratitude as an American citizen" be demonstrated better by engaging in the struggle to end those systems that oppress and destroy persons? From the standpoint of women's liberation, questions could be raised about male chauvinism and the way women have been used again and again to serve all kinds of male policy for "justifiable" reasons.

The young woman's quandary is a typical situation eth-

---

5. Joseph Fletcher, *Situation Ethics* (Philadelphia: The Westminster Press, 1966), p. 110.
6. Ibid., p. 164.

ics illustration. The situation was set forth in terms of a simplistic choice. The fact that sexual integrity was balanced against serving military intelligence implies that if she had decided to serve the military it would have been a loving choice (love of country) and therefore good. The system as such is accepted and hallowed by confusing it with love of country and with a good ethical decision. Because there was no analysis of the military system or nationalism there was no need for repentance by the young woman or the author for supporting these systems and the violence for which the systems are responsible. There is thus a false optimism about choices made in such a narrow interpretation of the situation. Professor Fletcher describes another such loving choice, which from a rules ethics might be wrong, by saying, "It is not excusably evil, it is positively good."[7]

Opposition to legalism, important as it is, is not the primary concern either of ethics or of Christian ethics. The primary concern is persons and the goal is liberation. The situation ethicist seems to be more interested in emancipating people from legalism than from structures of violence, on the assumption that the chief slavery or oppression today is a middle-class torture about temptations to violate ancient codes against killing and adultery. He fails to note that the chief victims of "justified" killing and sexual promiscuity are the poor, the minorities, and enemy people. There is also less legalism and therefore less guilt among the oppressed, with the result that situation ethics tends to become bourgeois license to function "ethically" as individuals within systems of oppression.

Liberation ethics neither relies on rules nor abstracts the principle of love from the New Testament. Instead it emphasizes a redemptive or liberating style of life made evident preeminently in the activity of Jesus but also demonstrated in the social action of Mohandas Gandhi, Martin

7. Ibid., p. 65.

Luther King, and others who gave their lives for human liberation. That style of life is so concerned with the affirmation of others, that it reveals the intimate connection between the paying of a personal price and the liberation of others. It indicates that love is sentimental if there is not the commitment to suffering for others which distinguishes it from self-indulgence. The willingness to suffer for the liberation of others is directly related to an unwillingness to inflict suffering on others. The old saying "hate the sin but love the sinner" approximated, without the knowledge of modern sociology, the idea that it is the system rather than the administrators of the system that must be eliminated. The refusal to inflict more violence on those caught in the system is not based on some rule that one must never injure another, but on an orientation or attitude of respect for others and a recognition that the real enemies are the systems that demean and dehumanize all of us.

Another major difference between liberation ethics and both rules and situation ethics is related to their respective understanding of history. Rules ethics, for example, approaches the problem of modern war from the standpoint of the rules or criteria of a "just war" which were formulated in the middle ages. These were intended not only as criteria for determining support of a given war but also as a restraint on the conduct of war. Those devoted to a rules ethics tend to try to fit new developments into ancient rules. They assert that the rules used by the medieval church to restrain the conduct of war can be used by churchmen today as a restraint on government leaders in the conduct of war. But even the tremendous church opposition to the war in Vietnam never succeeded in stopping the torture, saturation bombing, crop destruction, and other military tactics which were contrary to the "just war" criteria. "Just war" churchmen were more successful when they joined with pacifists and other antiwar voices in opposition to the war itself.

War as a system involves advanced technology which is

not susceptible to restraint. It is feasible, under certain circumstances when two or more nuclear powers are not engaged in a crucial struggle with each other, to avoid the use of nuclear weapons. However, no nuclear power has yet adopted a policy of restraint such as waging war by conventional means against an adversary using thermonuclear weapons. It is more realistic to advocate the unilateral abandonment of nuclear weapons prior to war than to urge restraint after the war has begun. The "just war" ethicists who are beguiled by rules of the past still advocate restraint during war rather than eliminating the system, in spite of the realities of contemporary weaponry and their knowledge of the nature of man. Man's nature is such that if he is not persuaded to eliminate weapons of mass destruction prior to war, he is not likely to withhold their use when losing or when others resort to them. The weapons used in a given war are not determined by the religious convictions or morality of churchmen. They are determined by the weapons technology available for use which were produced and stockpiled largely without protest from "just war" or rules ethicists.

Liberation ethics recognizes from historical developments that war is not likely to be waged on a level below that to which weapons technology has advanced unless enemy technology is inferior and such warfare serves the national interest. The saving of life and property is not dependent on the morality of individual men in the heat of war but on dealing with the system of war and its allied structures such as national military establishments, war industries, and imperialism. Unless these can be eliminated, rules for waging war with restraint are no answer to the problem. Instead they are a rationale to sustain the war system because they create the illusion that war can be made relatively moral.

Those who advocate situation ethics also accept a "just war" position because each war is different and must be supported or resisted according to the situation. They therefore support the war system so that it is available if there is a just war in the offing. The situationists' problem of history, however, is not with the rules of the past but with the failure to take history seriously. They do not seem to be clear about the meaning of the term *situation*. Sometimes it seems related to a larger context but more often situation ethics is distinguished from contextual ethics by appearing to be confined to a relatively short period of time in which a decision has to be made. It thus appears to concentrate on immediate facts to the exclusion of a larger context. One example used by Fletcher in his *Situation Ethics* indicates that President Harry Truman made his decision to atom-bomb Japanese civilians as a love calculation.[8] When *Situation Ethics* was written it was long known that Truman's decision was made after Japan had offered surrender with no conditions except the continuance of the emperor system. Prior to using the atom bombs, Truman insisted on the unconditional surrender of Japan. After the bombing, the Truman administration approved the continuance of the emperor, even though indicating he would be subject to the Allied commander. The bombs were not necessary for still another reason. General H. H. Arnold, chief of the U.S. Air Force, wrote in his third report that "no invasion was necessary"; neither did the "fall of the atomic bombs . . . cause the defeat of Japan . . ." It was the superiority of the U.S. Air Force that could bomb at will any city in Japan. The bombs were not necessary for Japanese surrender but they may have been deemed necessary to knock Japan out of the war before the Soviet Union could join the conquest of Asia and therefore participate in the postwar rule of conquered territory. There is some evidence that the bombs were dropped as a part of a power struggle the United States military leaders expected would develop with Russia and were therefore a

8. Ibid., p. 98.

warning to the USSR. The Truman administration's propaganda of the moment, that it was concerned with saving the lives of invading American soldiers, was nevertheless taken at face value and used as an illustration of situation ethics. It would be difficult for anyone committed to liberation to justify the mass destruction of others on the basis of parochial love for a group of invading soldiers. It would have been more appropriate to have encouraged active negotiations with the Japanese emperor and civilian leaders through neutral nations so as to avoid either Russian entry into the war or further destruction by the United States. Above all neither liberation nor love should be a mask for justifying the supremacy of one nation over another.

Such a situational illustration not only omitted the much more complex historical background of a developing rivalry with the USSR in Europe and the symbolic importance of the emperor in Japanese history, but it seemed to disregard the future. Liberation ethics depends a great deal on historical and political analyses as a factor in making decisions. It also holds that each incident is not confined to the specific persons involved, but exerts influence on others, whether as example or in changed attitudes, influence, or the like. The atom bombs dropped on Japan had a great impact on Soviet-American postwar relations, on developments in China, Japan, and on the arms race.

There is also a sociological difference between situation ethics and liberation ethics. Situation ethics contributes two basic ideas to the discipline of social ethics: (1) a concentration on immediate phenomena rather than on long range goals or strategies; and (2) utilitarianism—the idea that decisions are to be made on the basis of the greatest good for the greatest number of neighbors in need.

The concentration on immediate phenomena is supplemented by a rejection of ideology. Fletcher applies this specifically to war in his comment that a situationist could not be a pacifist or a militarist; he can only "stand for selective conscience."[9] By this he apparently means that it is impossible for a situationist to object to a whole pattern of action such as warfare or racial discrimination. One can only object to a specific war or a specific instance of racial discrimination because war and presumably discrimination are not in themselves right or wrong. But by the same token, the situationist apparently does not see warfare or segregation as social problems to be solved. Anyone who seeks planned social change must develop strategies for change, and strategy presupposes some theory of a better society as well as proximate goals that lead to it. But this is one meaning of ideology—a theory or hypothesis about a human or social problem with a strategy or approach for dealing with it. Professor Fletcher concludes that "in the end there is nothing but process." By this he evidently means unplanned process. Theologically this means that history has no goal.

Liberation ethics, however, believes that the goal of history is a community of men and women—a community that will have been liberated from war, racism, poverty, imperialism, and other major structures of violence. That liberation is not achieved by individuals making loving choices in specific situations but by the elimination or transformation of systems. On the other hand, systems are not likely to be changed by those who have no concern for their fellows. The point at issue is that systems are transformed by human beings as a result of successful strategies of social change as well as by a multiplicity of acts that have no intentional human relation to a specific goal. Such a multiplicity of acts which eventuate in social change are seen by Marxists as the development of history and by Christians and Jews as guided by God.

Liberation ethics recognizes that those who, as a matter of conviction or principle, oppose all forms of imperialism

9. Harvey Cox, ed., *The Situation Ethics Debate* (Philadelphia: The Westminster Press, 1968), p. 263.

or racism or war, make a significant contribution to social change. In practice the fact of conscientious objection to all war has made selective objection more possible. The pioneer work of conscientious objectors to all war not only led to the first congressional recognition of conscientious objection, but also to the first support for selective objectors.[10] In a typical midwestern city where conscientious objection of any type has not been popular, a certain college drop-out, George ———, had decided in 1967 to become a selective objector to the war in Vietnam. His entire family disapproved and there was no real understanding in his church or in other groups with which he was connected. He learned of the existence of a small Quaker meeting and then of a man who had been a conscientious objector in World War II. This man, now a teacher, had continued to read pacifist periodicals and served as a local draft counselor. George discovered during their conversation that he was not prepared to oppose all war and could not legally qualify for alternative service under the draft law. A Quaker lawyer took George's case without fee. Then George discovered a small but helpful group of pacifists in that city who stood with him in court, helped his family understand, and intervened to help in arranging parole when his father died while George was in prison. George did not change his fundamental position with respect to war, but he found that his own actions against a particular war would have been far less effective without the organization and support of those who held a principled position against all war.

The insistence that only situational judgment or selective conscience is valid with respect to such major social evils as war is as dogmatic as the idea that only an absolute rejection of such evils is valid. Certainly the insistence on

10. The first article in the *Christian Century* endorsing selective objection, and the first proposal in the American Civil Liberties Union for support of selective objectors came from long-term pacifists.

the validity of only situational judgments tends to be a
bulwark for the status quo. If consistent opposition to war
or racial inequality or to any social evil is rejected as
"ideological," then situation ethicists perforce accept the
necessity of national military machines without which war
cannot be waged. They likewise must accept some structures of racial inequality and other major social evils such
as imperialism, monopoly, and dictatorship. The freeing of
men from such structures on the assumption that they
constitute in themselves a form of bondage is a key aspect
of liberation ethics.

It is impossible logically to dismiss consistent opposition
to one social evil—war—as "ideological" and at the same
time to claim that principled opposition to another social
evil—racial segregation—is non-ideological. If the advocates of black power or nonviolence or socialism do make
a contribution to human freedom, then there may be a
place for ideology as a base for social strategies or for
symbolic principled witness that stirs others to strategic
decisions.

Another point of difference between situation ethics and
liberation ethics is utilitarianism. Fletcher emphasizes the
idea of the greatest good for the greatest number of neighbors in need. This tends to mean that alternate needs requiring action are finally decided by numbers. If a choice
has to be made between aiding a majority of poor whites or
a minority of poor blacks, those concerned with liberation
would probably say that the intensity of need and the
symbolic value of the smaller group should take priority. It
is even possible that the intensity of need of one person
may at a given moment preempt our social action; if that
one person's needs are met it may set a precedent or pattern for others. When we speak of liberation, however, the
issue is not determined by numbers but by the fact of
oppression. The existence of oppression is generally not
caused by an individual tyrant but is the result of systems
or practices which are accepted by both oppressors and

oppressed. These systems have a deleterious effect on both groups whether or not they are fully aware of it. The belief that numbers of people, perhaps an entire world, could be liberated by the killing of one man can easily flow from the idea that a real or symbolic oppressor must be destroyed. Situationists have created the impression that under such a circumstance the assassination of a tyrant would be in order. A number of situationists have referred to the significance of Dietrich Bonhoeffer's participation in the attempted assassination of Hitler as an act of love for the oppressed people of Germany, particularly since Bonhoeffer risked his life. As we shall observe in chapter eight, Bonhoeffer, however much he may have been motivated by love, was sadly lacking in political analysis. To assume that the assassination of Hitler would destroy nazism or Prussian militarism was to overlook the powerful military and political factors in Germany that had created Hitler and made him their spokesman. It is more than likely that the wounding or killing of Hitler would have made him a martyr to millions of Germans, creating a legend comparable to one following World War I, that Germany was defeated by internal betrayal, not by the wrongness of her cause or the superiority of the enemy. When one reads the commendation by situation ethicists of illustrations such as the abortive Bonhoeffer attempt at assassination, the net impression is that in comparable situations, tyrranicide is evidence of love. Yet such justification of assassination, if applied to southern governors who are articulate defenders of brutal systems of racial segregation, would not end segregation, any more than the assassination of a racist prime minister of South Africa changed things for the better in that country. In fact, the assassination of Julius Caesar, of Becket, and numerous other persons who were adjudged obstacles to civilization, did not work out as the assassins hoped. Social ethics requires careful analysis of history and the structures of society, not merely a devotion to love of one or more of its members.

The emphasis in liberation ethics is on transforming the system rather than on indicting or killing a few oppressors or servants of the system. Situation ethics by contrast uses illustrations that deal with personal relations where it seems advisable for the individual to act contrary to the rules to which church or society give lip service. The foregoing illustrations have involved the use of violence, including killing, or extramarital sexual relations, etc., as a way in which love is to be expressed in a particular situation. It could be assumed or deduced from the antilegalist approach of the New Testament that there may be situations in which killing or adultery or false witness are required by love, but such situations are not used to illustrate what is meant by love. It is significant that the illustrations used by Jesus provide an orientation of respect for life, rather than a set of suggestions for each of a number of situations where it would be permissible or loving to injure or kill others or to destroy family or community relationships. When Jesus broke the Sabbath law, for example, it was in the interest of sustaining and enhancing life. When he attacked legalism it was to advance respect for persons. "You have heard it said, 'An eye for an eye and a tooth for a tooth.' But I say to you . . ."

The issue today does not seem to involve a dispute between a rules ethics or a system that completely repudiates rules. There seems to be little question that situation ethics has served as a corrective to the popular assumption that ethics depends on biblical or other rules. It also has immense value for counseling because it helps people see possible courses of action that might be the best for them in a given situation. This, however, as Thomas Russell suggests, is a narrow model and the difficulty arises not when it is used by one individual in an isolated situation "but when it is applied to far more comprehensive situations. A decision reached by counsellor and counselee after many serious questions is quite another matter than having the same conclusion published in the newspaper as general

advice."[11] The issue today is whether it is possible to have
an ethical methodology without rules that is prescriptive
enough to give real direction to conduct. The answer to
that question is that ethics should be based on redemption,
which has already been defined as liberating persons from
whatever it is that enslaves them. According to liberation
ethics, anything is good if it functions redemptively and
bad if it does not. To function redemptively means paying
a price ourselves to set men free. It does not mean injuring
or enslaving some men to set others free. When we are
agents of liberation we are not at the same time agents of
oppression or death.

Perhaps the most obvious problem in American society
is that of racial oppression. Liberation ethics starts with the
assumption that the enormous structure of violence erected
by white men to subjugate black men cannot be eliminated
by the mere adoption of laws or by well-developed rules of
morality. Neither can it be dealt with by loving action,
situation by situation.

The liberation of black people requires the successful
elimination of segregation and white racism. This cannot
be done unless a number of whites and blacks pay a price
and pay it willingly. Martin Luther King rightly indicated
that blacks had to pay a price not only to liberate black
men but also to redeem white men from their terrible sin
against their brothers. But no white man can ask any black
man to pay that price even though black freedom may
require black leadership that also is concerned about the
white adversaries. White suggestions that blacks should be
loving or nonviolent carry too many implications of white
vested interests, especially if the same advice is not given to
affluent whites who profit from the systems of oppression.

On the other hand it is essential for all concerned with
liberation to note that there are no guarantees of success

11. Rev. Thomas Russell to author, 19 April 1969, Kahoka,
Missouri.

either for violent or nonviolent movements. The crucifixion of Jesus, the assassinations of Gandhi and King; and the power struggles and repression in which Stalin, Mao, and others have been involved, all demonstrate that success is neither immediate nor certain. Paradoxically, oppression is more likely to be ended by those who renounce political or economic control for themselves than by those who seek to gain such dominance. The former keep themselves free from the possibility of using their newly acquired power to maintain it at the expense of others. This is one reason that liberation is more clearly associated with leaders such as Jesus, Gandhi, and King, who renounced control of others, than with Stalin, Mao, or other political rulers who promised the ending of oppression. The other reason is that liberation of an enemy is an integral part of achieving freedom for oneself. It is the system that enslaves both. It is impossible, however, for rulers concerned with their own power willingly to pay a price for others. Their practice is to make others pay a price for them. They tend, therefore, to increase both the dehumanization of men and the power of evil.

Liberation ethics recognizes the great power of evil in the world and in ourselves and therefore acknowledges that there is no easy strategy to make men happy or to set them free. We are set free only when those who love us pay a price.

3

OPPRESSION AND THE STRUCTURES OF VIOLENCE

VIOLENCE CAN BE defined in many ways. A lawyer would probably define it as the unlawful use of force, but such a definition would not get to the heart of the problem, since law in every society is written, administered, and interpreted by those who are in a position to exploit the minority, the poor, and the powerless. A Marxist, on the other hand, would think of any social order other than a socialist society as being inherently violent because the instruments of violence such as the police, the army, and the courts are used to maintain the position and privileges of the middle and upper classes.

It is also possible to define violence by the injury that occurs when force is directed against human beings. The gunman who pistol-whips and robs another man engages in violence, not because his actions are unlawful, but because someone is hurt. The policeman who shoots and arrests the gunman uses violence even though he acts within the law. The same officer of the law two hours earlier may have captured a valuable animal that escaped from the zoo. In that case he probably used a tranquilizing dart that took the same amount of time to demobilize the animal as the bullet did with the man. The comparison may suggest that nonlethal weapons technology should be perfected for human offenders against the law, but it also spotlights the violence now lawfully used against people. This violence has also been directed at persons who have committed no crimes but simply appear suspicious, as a running black man does to white police or to National Guardsmen in the course of violent disturbances in the black ghetto. Yet he may have been running for any number of lawful reasons.

In our society there are at least two types of violence. The overt type which is immediately visible includes crime, riots, war, revolution, counterrevolution, and usually involves the use of weapons to injure or kill human beings. The covert type is hidden from the general population, frequently in myths of patriotism or law-and-order. The covert type is violence that has been institutionalized in various systems or structures which keep people from being free. These systems or structures of violence are generally reinforced by police action against those who resist the system. This often occurs even when resistance is nonviolent. The term *oppression* is not synonymous with specific acts of overt violence, but is embodied in the continued denial of freedom or dignity or security that is characteristic of the systems of violence in our society.

Conscription is a system of violence that is covert because it has been institutionalized and legitimized. It became acceptable to many people who were led to believe it was necessary for national defense. Yet the violence to a family when a teen-age son is taken away from home, against his will, to be trained for war may be as great as the violence done by kidnapping. In each case there is forced separation of a person from his family, continuing loss of freedom, and continuing physical danger.

Conscription also has a collective impact on the nation which can be described as institutionalized or systemic violence. Lewis Mumford called it the "systematic regimentation of a whole population . . ." Through conscription the "army became in effect an educational institution for conditioning its human units" to the acceptance of armed violence and national military policy, including "ideological doctrines and emotional responses."[1]

The oppression of conscription is maintained by the FBI which arrests those who refuse to be drafted and by the army after a boy has been processed and inducted. It is maintained also by well-publicized but false myths that it is the most equitable way of raising manpower or that civilians rotated through the arm periodically will prevent a professional army.

Racial segregation is another illustration of violence. It is covert because it was institutionalized centuries ago and accepted by whites as a part of the American way of life. Many whites are not aware of the physical and personality damage that occurs to people living in the black ghetto because of hunger, crowded conditions, miserable housing, proximity to rats, and little if any creative recreation. It is the unusual white teacher or parent who helps his children to examine the black ghetto critically or to understand sympathetically the need of its inhabitants for liberation. A white newspaper reporter visiting Syracuse, New York, in 1971 after some racial clashes asked a black leader "if blacks enjoyed the camping, boating, fishing and skiing that the whites [he had] interviewed had praised." The black leader replied: "Close to 25 percent of the black population is on welfare and 40 percent of the population is at or below the poverty level. While whites are whipping out to the lakes, we're just trying to survive."[2] Another black leader indicated that the white experience is so different that whites are convinced "black people or poor people simply need to work hard to succeed."[3]

1. Lewis Mumford, *The Myth of the Machine, The Pentagon of Power* (New York: Harcourt Brace Jovanovich, Inc., 1970), p. 240.
2. *New York Times*, 11 August 1971.
3. Ibid.

The oppression of the ghetto is maintained by a combination of factors. Living in the ghetto with little contact with whites and with segregated or poorer education makes it difficult to get any except menial jobs. There is consequently no money with which to move out of the ghetto. In addition, white bankers and real estate firms make mortgage loans difficult or impossible for blacks who want to live outside of the ghetto. Frequently there is overt violence or threat of violence from whites if blacks think of new housing areas. The following is an account of a reporter's interview with the director of human relations in Syracuse, New York, a city of 196,000 people. The report indicated that in 1970

the United Task Force Development Corporation, a black business and professional organization, tried to build some 225 homes on 95 acres "of the Rand tract" a short distance from the border of a black area in the southern section of Syracuse. The venture . . . would have brought more costly homes and higher salaried black residents into the area than the whites who now live there.

"We met with whites from the area in the Valley Presbyterian Church to ask their cooperation," he [the director of human relations] said, "and they told us 'if you build it, we'll burn it down.' The police had to come and escort us out of it. The whites were just that hostile." The plan was not carried through. . . .[4]

The violence of the segregation system and of racism is not exclusively turned against blacks. Low-income black residents pushing into marginal "white areas" have frequently had little concern either for the persons or the property of white old-age pensioners or other whites with too little income to flee to the suburbs.

Poverty is another structure of violence. It is unnecessary in our present stage of technological development. It

4. Ibid.

also enslaves men to their physical requirements, often torturing them with hunger and disease. In other words, it keeps them from realizing their own true worth and therefore dehumanizes them. Many people believe that poverty is caused by laziness, lack of initiative or lack of ability. In some cases this is undoubtedly true. On the other hand, there are people with both intelligence and physical strength who have been born into a village in India or Bolivia or Mississippi where there are few if any educational opportunities. They may have been conditioned by centuries of realization that their color or caste or other circumstances dooms them to menial types of work at low pay from which they can never escape. They may even give up trying very hard because they know that whatever they do, life will not be much better or worse for them.

Still others live in poverty because of the way they are manipulated by systems. When the Nixon administration decided to fight inflation it had a choice of imposing an excess profits tax on industry, including price and wage controls, or of lowering purchasing power by stimulating more unemployment. On October 7, 1969, Secretary of Treasury David Kennedy told Congress that a four percent unemployment rate was "acceptable" to the administration in its fight against inflation and it might even be necessary to have a higher rate. The rate did in fact go above six percent in 1970 and 1971. Those among the unemployed who were eager for work were victims of that approach of fighting inflation which maintained the high profits of industry.

The evidence that the system is responsible for poverty may be seen from an unpublished study by Bernard Pyron. He discovered that in March 1961 during the worst of a recession there were "525,000 families on general relief and in January 1966 there were "fewer than 300,000 families on general relief." At least 200,000 families apparently got off "relief" by taking jobs as they became available. There is an interrelationship of systems with the result that some poverty is caused or increased by other systems such as racial segregation or war or a medical system geared to ability to pay high costs. High medical and hospital costs together with a relatively long illness of any of its members can drive a middle class family into poverty. The pollution of land and water can cause poverty or unemployment for farmers, fishermen, or others. Military conscription in the United States and elsewhere has been basically a way of getting cheap manpower for the armed forces. Those who entered because they wanted a career in the military also suffered from depressed wages because of the draft. An Air Force survey completed in 1964 revealed that 71,000 Air Force personnel were engaged in off-duty jobs to supplement their income and an additional 5,000 Air Force personnel were receiving some form of relief benefits for the poor. The President's Commission on an All Volunteer Armed Force headed by former Secretary of Defense Thomas Gates reported in 1970 that young men who were drafted received less in pay and services than they could have earned in a civilian job and less than the amount required to induce them to volunteer. The difference of $3,600 per man on an average represented an annual tax on these men and their families. The various powerful systems under which people live can and do result in oppression. This is accentuated when people feel the full impact of a number of such systems at the same time.

A complex society is a network of educational, religious, industrial, financial, political, military, racial, and other systems. Some of these structures of society are beneficial, or partly helpful and partly oppressive.

The oppressive structures or systems (as well as the others) have generally grown or evolved over a long period of time, so that the originators of human slavery or monopoly capitalism or war are no longer present to be punished or converted into opponents of the systems they originated. In a primitive society it might be easy to identify the few "strong men" who were responsible for the oppression of the poor and the powerless. In a complex society, on the other hand, the various systems are administered or defended not only by their enthusiastic supporters but also by those who have misgivings about them and by those who have never analyzed the relation of these systems to the oppression of others. For example, the police who defend the status quo, including white power, against any potential or actual black threats to the existing order, do not make the basic decisions that maintain racism in our society. They do not determine the educational, employment, housing, or mortgage loan policies that help perpetuate segregation. The police receive their orders from others who in turn do not have the sole power to change the system. The police are generally drawn from lower income groups and with few exceptions earn low wages. They are thus often living at a level of poverty or not far above the poverty line. Their status and function as police officers in spite of their lack of economic or political power is what makes them seem to others as among the oppressors rather than among the oppressed.

It is essential to recognize that in a complex society, systems rather than individuals are the root of oppression. No one man or group is responsible in the sense that his or their elimination would cause the whole oppressive structure to collapse. The war system is a case in point. If every general, admiral, and the heads of corporations that comprise the military industrial complex were killed because they involved the nation in an unpopular war, it would not eliminate the war system. That system will continue so long as most of the people are still persuaded that national armies, navies, and air forces defend values they hold dear or are necessary for employment or prosperity or to maintain the political and economic structures they accept.

Liberation ethics is concerned about systems because these are the realities of a complex society, but also because those who think of individuals, groups or classes as their oppressors engage in too simplistic an analysis of the enemy. The structures of oppression cannot be eliminated by destroying those who administer them or profit from them. The rich and the powerful who are or seem to be on top are not usually self-made men but the product of many persons who have willingly and unwillingly assisted them in reaching and maintaining their position. The executives and major stockholders of General Motors maintain their salaries and profits in spite of the production of unsatisfactory cars because millions of middle- and lower-class people buy their products. Presidents, governors, and political parties are supported by ordinary citizens in spite of the fact that they do almost nothing to provide adequate health facilities, education, housing, and income for the millions of unemployed and low-income families who vote for them. Both the economic and political systems of the United States are dependent on the continued support of millions of people. The poor, both white and black, are oppressed and at the same time support the systems which oppress them. Every system continues only with their support.

If we blame an elite group for oppression then it is unnecessary to change the system. All that is required is a power shift that will put in power a properly motivated elite. It has not been possible to eliminate elites or the ruling class, as Marx assumed in his goal of a classless society, nor has it been possible to put in power representatives of the proletarian class or any group forever friendly to it. In any complex industrial society there will be bureaucrats or technologists or managers who administer the systems under which men live. Even if there is no obvious owning group these managers of the systems become the elite, conscious of their power and privileges. They do not transcend the structures they have inherited, such as the industrial system, or war, or the myths of nationalism.

There are suprapersonal and perhaps suprahuman elements involved in every structure that oppresses people. These elements are not cosmic, comparable to the ancient belief that the stars or some supernatural demons control men for evil. They are structures which men have collectively erected and which have attained a dynamism of their own. The machines invented by men have led to a kind of technical autonomy. If man makes use of machines or of weapons or of war there are certain functional rules which he must follow. Man's hopes or wishes amount to nothing once the machine or the system is set in motion. The machine, in all of its progressive changes from manual operation to automation and cybernation, conditions or changes the social, political, and economic situation. The political scene, for example, does not determine the way the machine operates nor the technological evolution into cybernation. It may for a time disrupt production or technological evolution through the interference of war, revolution, or other political events, but all politics have to reckon with suprapersonal and suprahuman systems that have a momentum or dynamism of their own.

The idea that the systems under which we live are in part created by forces at work in the world which we cannot control is deeply imbedded in two of the leading modern systems of thought, Marxism and Christianity. The Marxist concept of historical materialism holds that the developments of history are not the result of free decisions on the part of groups and individuals to change their way of life, but the result of economic developments that compelled change. The Polish Marxist philosopher, Adam Schaff, adds that "Marxist determinism understands historical necessity not as a force acting on society from outside, independent of society, but as operating precisely through human actions. . . . What we call necessity is nothing else than the sum of a tremendous number of individual events."[5]

Hebrew and Christian thought has similarly held that

5. Adam Schaff, *A Philosophy of Man* (New York: Dell, 1968), p. 72.

there are suprapersonal forces which either pervert or help shape history. Evil has been personified or symbolized in demonic forces in both Jewish and Christian writings. The apostle Paul, however, had a very sophisticated view of systems such as the law, or public opinion, or tradition, which dominated men. His sophistication is evident in that he did not view men simply as separate entities who yielded to specific sins or vices but instead saw that men inherited certain structures of existence. These structures may originally have had a good purpose of holding life together, in much the same way as law serves a useful purpose but can be perverted into an instrument of oppression. He saw these structures, rather than evil men, as the enemy that must be fought. So he said that "our fight is not against any physical enemy; it is against organizations and powers . . ."[6] Another translation of the same statement says "for ours is not a conflict with mere flesh and blood but with the despotisms, the empires, the forces that control and govern . . ."[7]

It would be difficult in our modern world, even if one rejects these Marxist or Christian assumptions, to demonstrate that systems are simply dependent on a few groups or individuals whose elimination would thereby destroy or transform a given social structure.[8]

A. J. Muste wrote that "a 'system' is just human beings living in certain relationships and unless something happens in the human being nothing has happened at all."[9] Muste's point was that human acquiescence in or support of systems required change. Unless this happens at a deep

6. *Eph.* 6:12, J. B. Phillips, trans.
7. Weymouth Translation
8. Leninists and Maoists, who have modified or changed Marxist doctrine, believe in the physical destruction of opponents, but Marx never held that the destruction of persons is the key factor in transforming systems.
9. A. J. Muste, "The Situation and Program of Christianity," *Religion in Life* (Spring 1939), pp. 223–24.

rather than superficial level the old system continues in one form or another after the administrators of the system have been changed. The mere fact that a group of socialists is antiimperialist or antiwar prior to a revolution does not result in an end to imperialism or the war system following the revolution. There is a tendency in all revolutions to continue the major practices of the old structures, partly because those structures are suprapersonal and cannot be eliminated by eliminating their administrators and defenders, and partly because the parents, teachers and other leaders of the "new" society have not been transformed intellectually or in their wills so that their commitment is to a genuinely liberated community.

The fact that oppressive systems must be eliminated or transformed necessarily requires conflict. There is an inevitability of conflict as long as there are oppressed groups seeking change. Conflict arises whenever there are groups or classes or races whose collective future depends on liberation from systems which operate in the interest of other groups. Karl Marx brilliantly but too simplistically saw conflict only in economic class terms: the interest of the workers was in low prices and high wages, whereas the employer's interest was served by high prices and low wages. This idea of a fundamental contradiction of interests necessarily has been broadened to include any groups whose oppression has been institutionalized by military, political, racial, cultural, or other systems. This contradiction of interests is most evident in the recent conflict between such groups as black militants and white supremacists, antiwar demonstrators and veterans organizations, but it is also present at other points. When such group conflict erupts against a system or its adherents it generally also directs its energies against the government.

Theoretically democratic governments are responsive to these conflicts and seek to arbitrate them or resolve them by modifying the most oppressive systems. Labor unions were finally legitimized in the 1930s in the United States and given a modest stake in the society in order to avoid serious conflict between the capitalist system and the urban workers. But some systems are so entrenched and so integral to the U.S. government that little if any yielding is likely by the government except after the most serious conflict. Examples of such entrenched systems are monopoly capitalism and the military.

From one point of view slight modification of any system is an improvement, especially if modifications can be produced again and again. But from another point of view, minor improvements in any system are substitutes for real change intended to make the status quo tolerable. In this way the primary administrators and beneficiaries of any system can contribute to the system's own resistance to major change. Anything that is intended to perpetuate a system of violence and thus forestall or delay liberation is itself a form of violence.

Liberation is the opposite of making the status quo tolerable. It assumes the validity of eliminating or transforming structures that oppress, rather than giving some of the oppressed more of a stake in the system. In this respect liberation ethics also rejects certain strategies of justice such as the "balance-of-power" theory which Reinhold Niebuhr and many other political liberals have pushed so vigorously. According to this theory, power combinations should be used or formed to balance or check other power groups. If capitalists are strong, labor unions should be strengthened to forestall or prevent too much power on the part of capital. If the military-industrial complex is too strong, it is essential to build either a strong consumer-industrial complex or to build a strong antiwar movement in order to achieve some equilibrium. A reasonable equilibrium, it is said, is the basis for a pluralist society.

There is a sense in which the balance-of-power model seems to lead to liberation. If any group or person is powerless while others are powerful there is bound to be oppression. Therefore, the acquisition of power is equated with the elimination of oppression. The truth in this idea is that weakness invites oppression. But it is also possible to be physically or financially or politically strong and still be oppressed. The apparently powerful conscript armies of Hitler, Stalin, Roosevelt, and their successors were not free. The apparently strong labor unions in the United States do not have real strength. Taxation falls more heavily on workers and conscription more heavily on their children than on the financiers and industrialists. Actually by giving labor a minor share in the system the unions have been co-opted so that they are no longer the champions of the exploited and seldom attempt to counterbalance the power of government or industry.

From the standpoint of the oppressed, liberation may seem to take place when they have acquired a position of strength so that they are less vulnerable to exploitation. But this seeming strength suggests a second fallacy in the balance-of-power idea. This is the fact that there are no genuine balances—no equilibrium based on power. Groups or interests that seek financial or military or political strength are not content with an exact balance, because such balances checkmate each other rather than facilitate movement toward greater freedom. The oppressed group that begins with seeking a balance of power either goes on to seek greater strength than the oppressing group or finally yields the struggle to accept a subordinate role. An antiwar movement that is willing to share power with or be the "loyal opposition" to the military-industrial complex ceases to be a real force for peace. It must seek the elimination of that complex or become its captive.

The balance-of-power model also assumes that large groups of like-minded people can achieve enough strength to check the power of other groups so as to achieve a relative freedom from their control. But men and women may belong to such a power group for one reason and find themselves out of harmony with the group for another reason. A labor union, for example, may exist to check the power of one or more employers yet be bound to an ostensibly prolabor government and a war which that government is waging. A minority within the union may know that the war has been pushed by financial interests or the military-industrial complex and yet be shorn of their freedom to oppose the war, or the government which at some points provides benefits for the union.

Black power faces a similar problem. The more some black people get real economic power and real status in white America, the less identity they will have with the lower-class black masses. Black community power to bargain with white power is better than no power at all. But what is needed is liberation from racism, not the kind of bargaining power labor unions have achieved with specific industries in an otherwise unchanged economic system.

The idea advanced by some people that the way to deal with the military-industrial complex is by building up the power of a consumer-industrial complex is symptomatic of those who use the balance-of-power approach. The military-industrial complex is so pervasive in its contracting and subcontracting that the major consumer industries receive from five to thirty-five or more percent of their income from the military. Frequently people are misled into thinking that power groups balance each other. They do not realize that apparently rival industries or political parties are often governed by the same interests or have working relationships on crucial issues.

In practice the balance-of-power approach is a program for making the status quo tolerable by affording the oppressed more of an ability to bargain with or associate with those who administer the major structures of society. This access to or relative acceptance by those in power may appease many of those who are less priviliged, but such relative acceptance must not be confused with liberation. Middle- and upper-class blacks and whites are still vulnerable to the catastrophe of war implicit in the military system, however much they may think they profit from it;

and as long as there is widespread racism in any society, black political and economic leaders will face, during times of racial conflict, the same repression experienced steadily by poor blacks.

Although the balance-of-power approach is not likely to contribute to liberation, increasing power as such in the hands of the poor, minorities, antiwar, and other groups is essential to ultimate liberation. Power resulting from organization and commitment to clear goals of liberation is different from that simply designed to provide some check on another group or gain a little bargaining power with the administrators of a system. Therefore the organization of welfare recipients, of the unemployed, the poor, the minorities, and coalitions of these groups will be necessary for the kind of creative conflict that is needed to transform systems of oppression.

In Latin America those who rationalize the systems of exploitation do not talk of the balance-of-power model. Instead they talk of development. This means the development of industry and agriculture so as to create more of a middle class and more of a stake in the system for a middle class. It does not mean either the creation of a counterbalancing opposition to North American industry or the elimination of poverty by the creation of a new economic system. Liberation, rather than development, has become the position of the oppressed and their intellectual leaders in Latin America. They have recognized the futility of waiting decades until current industrial systems are expanded to the point where some of the millions who live in poverty can be absorbed gradually into a middle class which will act as a buffer between the rich and the poor.

If neither the balance-of-power approach nor increased development is likely to prove liberating, there is still the democratic hope that the people by sheer voting power will liberate themselves.

Democracy means rule by the people, but real democracy does not exist in the United States. One of the chief aspects of American democracy is the election system. Elections, however, are controlled by political parties which offer no clear choices to the people. Men who run for office are not expected to keep promises made during an election campaign, as all recent presidents of the United States have demonstrated. People are encouraged to vote for men, not for meaningful political platforms or principles. In most cases presidents and other high federal and state officials must be wealthy or have easy access to wealth. Poor men do not become president or members of the cabinet or, with a very occasional exception, members of the House of Representatives. The costliness of running for office and the difficulty of being accepted by the influential men who lead political parties contribute to the control of the elections by those interests in American life that are associated with powerful systems. Those who are elected can achieve real influence only as they prove satisfactory over a long period of time to the major economic systems and their supporters. The committee system and the seniority system in Congress combine to put control of crucial measures into the hands of one man or relatively few men who have again and again been re-elected, often from districts controlled by special interests.

The other major aspect of American democracy is summarized under the phrase "freedom of association." This means that various business, professional, religious, labor, educational, and other interests organize, discuss, and plan strategy for advancing matters of concern to them. They employ lobbyists, publish periodicals, and engage in coalitions with groups not adversely affected by their program. The poor have the same right to organize as do the upper- and middle-income groups but they have little money, education, and energy at the close of a working day to devote to such organizations. They are also susceptible to propaganda and to public heroes who seem to be on their side.

There are consequently few groups that are organized to challenge the power of large business monopolies or professional monopolies such as the American Medical Association and the American Bar Association.

In the United States and most other countries the lower-income groups and those who are unemployed have little if any power or influence either politically or economically. Workers, whether clerks in investment or lending institutions, or operators of machinery, are hired and trained to perform a specific task needed by the company so that they have no participation in the decisions about the production process itself. The company views them as a kind of soldier whose wages, hours, quotas, and conditions of work are determined by the officers. The workers bargain for slightly higher wages but they have no participation in directing the company or organizing its production. The firm pays the workers a small part of the income they earn while management makes a maximum profit and joins other firms in reigning over civil society.

The essence of oppression is not necessarily hardship but the feeling of powerlessness which comes from knowing that the basic decisions are made for you and in spite of anything you do. The powerless include blacks segregated against their will, workers who have no say in the production process, conscripts who are forced to prepare for and fight wars, and students whose curriculum and academic environment are prescribed by the dominant systems of our society. If it is accurate to describe many of the systems of our society as oppressive, it is natural to ask what kind of society would be nonoppressive. Such a society would:

1. End all segregation and discrimination based on sex, race, religion, national origin, or economic position. This would include schools, housing, union membership, and employment, among others.
2. Involve cooperative ownership of the major means of production by workers or by workers and consumers or by

political communities; it would improve the position of farmers through the development of cooperatives for production, processing, and distribution of their products.

3. Abolish conscription and would join in an international agreement to abolish all armaments and armed forces or prepare for nonmilitary forms of defense. As a transition, armed forces and weapons would be reduced to the point that they could neither be used to invade nor to attack nations overseas.

4. Transform colleges and universities so that students and faculties jointly determine educational policies, including the employment of administrators and teachers.

5. Reorient the economy so as to include workers and consumers in planning for economic development, reconversion, and other financial policies.

6. Guarantee an adequate income, possibly through a negative income tax to all members of society. This would discourage the movement of farm families and farm youth into the cities for an adequate income.

7. Change the tax structure to avoid loopholes and discrimination.

8. Abandon imperialism, including military alliances and defense of overseas business investments and multinational corporations. In place of such empire, assurances could be given to relatively nonindustrialized nations of multinational planning and assistance in developing agriculture, industry, and public services and public capital.

9. Develop public services and facilities at little or no cost in areas of regular or continuing need such as health, transportation, cultural and athletic facilities and events, and child day-care centers.

10. Conserve natural and other resources by ending water, air, and land pollution and by producing for durability rather than for obsolescence. Products ranging from light bulbs to automobiles can be built to last rather than built to wear out after a short life.

The above list is intended to be suggestive rather than exhaustive. In all situations wherever possible there should be decentralized control of schools, production, and other services so as to avoid the pitfalls of both Communist dictatorship and capitalist monopoly control. Liberation is not to be achieved, however, by dreaming of some utopia, blueprinting it, and dogmatically insisting on its achievement. Liberation is dynamic and moves progressively to establish new programs as decision making is progressively transferred to the people. Political and economic liberation involves the eliminating of systems of oppression so that decision making is in the hands of decentralized communities. Such communities of neighbors or workers or educators or students must be built upon respect for the opinions and well being of all persons which necessarily means each person.

4

LIBERATION AND REVOLUTION

LIBERATION FROM THE STRUCTURES of violence requires fundamental social change which can only be described as revolutionary. The word *revolution*, however, is widely misunderstood. The political word *revolution* originally meant what the scientific term still means: a complete rotation which is in harmony with natural laws. The word *revolution* was applied to the English upheaval which involved the execution of Charles I, because at the end of the upheaval there was a return to the beginning point with the placing of Charles II on the throne. It could be argued that the contemporary implication of the term *revolution* is the same because it involves an overthrow of one group of oppressors and a return to oppression after the victors have had a chance to taste power. This may in fact be what has happened in many revolutions, but the contemporary intent is to achieve social change without a continuation of oppression. Therefore revolution does not mean the mere transfer of power from an oppressing to an oppressed group. Such a shift does not necessarily eliminate oppression.

Neither is a revolution the same as a coup d'état, which is generally the seizure of political control by one faction or set of administrators at the expense of another. Those who carry out the coup d'état are generally among the dominant groups in society rather than among the less powerful. From time to time a largely bloodless coup d'état occurs when the army or a part of it seizes power. In some of these cases, as in Egypt under Colonel Nasser and in Peru following the military coup of 1968, there is enough social change of benefit to the people that the entire process is considered revolutionary. However, a major obstacle to real revolution in such continuing military or elitist rule is paternalism or dictatorship. The social change occurs for the people and with little or any participation on their part.

Frequently revolution is identified with rapid or drastic social change, in contrast to evolution which implies change over a long period of time. Yet change that has occurred over decades can be revolutionary. The period when various types of machines were being developed and used has been called the Industrial Revolution solely because of the fundamental nature of the change and the transfer of power that accompanied it.

The fact that violence, especially massive violence, has been used in an effort to end oppression, has misled many people into thinking that a revolution is defined by violence and upheaval rather than by basic change. This idea that political violence is revolutionary has been reinforced by journalists and popular writers who called the violence in various countries the "Russian Revolution," or the "French Revolution," or the "Spanish Revolution," without waiting to evaluate the outcome or to see whether basic changes had taken place. Such names persist even when the most brutal use of power was directed by the successful "revolutionaries" against the people they promised to liberate. Only a few political writers have claimed that violence is really antirevolutionary. Bart de Ligt, a Dutch writer, argues that "the social revolution means nothing if it is not a battle for humanity against all that is inhuman and unworthy of man." That is why he insists that "the more there is of real revolution, the less there is of violence: the more of violence, the less of revolution."[1]

Violent revolution too often represents a mere transfer of power and oppression from one group to another. Karl Marx gave a better definition of revolution than such a transfer of power when he called it the transformation of an entire system. This has been spelled out by another writer as "a forced transfer of power within a nation from one class, group or individual to another . . . a transfer sufficiently permanent to enable those who have obtained possession of the State to make basic changes in the social, military and economic position of the several classes."[2] The phrase "forced transfer of power" does not necessarily imply violence, for the word *force* is defined simply as the generic use of energy. There have been revolutions in history accompanied by little or no violence on the part of the revolutionaries, and others where the destruction of life and property has been tremendous. On the other hand, revolution is impossible unless the existing social order is violent in its effect. Men simply do not revolt against humane systems or for theological or ideological reasons alone. The structures of society have to be sufficiently oppressive so as to inflict obvious violence on a substantial number of people.

Unfortunately history records transfers of power resulting in basic changes in the social, military, and economic systems which have not, however, resulted in a more humanizing society. In our day revolution refers to the liberation of men from one or more structures of violence by a process that results in enhancing or humanizing life. It

1. Bart de Ligt, *The Conquest of Violence* (New York: E. P. Dutton & Co., Inc., 1938), p. 162.
2. Robert Hunter, *Revolution: Why, How, When* (New York: Harper and Brothers, 1940), p. x.

involves a transfer of real decision making from an elite to the people. Revolution implies a new and liberating order as well as basic changes in the political and economic systems. If a revolution transforms one brutal system into another brutal system, as evident in the transition from tsarist Russia to Stalinist communism, it may be labeled as a revolution because of some basic changes in the political and economic systems. But if it is not humanizing or redemptive it is not an acceptable event to those who seek liberation. This means that the test of whether an event is revolutionary is not in the intentions of those who set it in motion, but in the end result—if it has in fact accomplished liberation. The intentions of men are insufficient. It is the meaning of the event as given by God or history.

The American Civil War was not a revolution, even though it resulted in the ending of human slavery in the United States. It was no longer legally possible to own slaves, but white men in the North as well as the South continued to treat black people as if they were still a form of property to be exploited. It was this continued degradation of persons that has produced the current demand for black liberation in the United States, more than one hundred years after the Civil War.

Neither was the so-called American Revolution a genuine revolution. It was a war of independence from England, but it did not result in a different political or economic system. The American myth frequently taught in both public and private schools is that the thirteen colonies were a subject people who had to fight the British in order to gain freedom from tyranny or control over their own lives. In reality there was an American ruling class made up largely of landed gentry, merchants, and yeomen from England who "with their psychology and social values were reproduced in a new environment."[3] These American rul-

3. Charles A. Beard and Mary R. Beard, *The Rise of American Civilization* (New York: Macmillan, 1930), p. 126.

ing classes made up the colonial assemblies or legislatures, since there were property qualifications for voting. They made the basic political and economic decisions, though there were attempts from England, after George III came to power, to retrieve some authority. The American ruling group "had already wrested the government from the royal authorities by 1765; their uprising was designed to preserve what they had rather than to gain something new and untried."[4]

At least ten years before the war the American colonists, or rather the propertied group, had consummated the bourgeois revolution that the French propertied and professional groups were to attempt about twenty-five years later. Charles and Mary Beard described the situation in the colonies as follows:

On the eve of the Revolution, the royal and proprietary governors, beggars at the door of the assemblies, were powerless to enforce by civil process their instructions from England; provincial councils had lost most of their control over law-making and judges and minor officers had to trim to the legislators to avoid putting their salaries in jeopardy. For practical purposes the colonial assemblies in their domestic concerns were their own masters and their strength was increasing. The revolution had actually taken place; nothing but an explosion was necessary to announce it to the world.[5]

The civil liberties enjoyed by Americans prior to the war were many as the Declaration of Independence indicates in listing the rights that were threatened. Those who wanted expansion of liberty for themselves organized more than a decade before the war to restrict the liberties of those who were suspected of being disloyal to their cause. The "Revolution" itself provided an excuse for denying liberty to minorities and dissenters. "But when the war emergency had passed, a dangerous precedent remained. The nature

4. Ibid., p. 187.
5. Ibid., p. 118.

and devices of the Revolution fixed in the popular mind a conception of *force majeure* acting for its self-conceived 'common good.' "[6] It was not until December 15, 1791 that the Bill of Rights was proclaimed in the form of amendments to the federal Constitution. These rights were broadly stated and had to be interpreted by court decisions over the years. But from the beginning the Bill of Rights was construed as restricting the federal government rather than the states from interfering with personal liberty. It was not until after the Civil War that states were forbidden to engage in slavery or "deprive any person of life, liberty, or property without due process of law. . . ." In 1925 the Supreme Court said the First Amendment's guarantee of freedom of speech and of the press were rights which the Fourteenth Amendment forbade the states to impair. Some other rights flowing from the first ten amendments to the federal Constitution have also been construed as applying with respect to the states. It is therefore possible to say that many if not most of the civil liberties enjoyed in the United States today by the poor, workers, minorities, and dissenters were achieved after 1933, many of them during the decade when Earl Warren was chief justice of the Supreme Court.

The War of Independence did not liberate the poor or indentured servants; neither did it grant them equality within the American system. Yet in various states and on the western frontier the people began to demand changes that paved the way for the era of Andrew Jackson beginning in 1828. During his administration a bloodless social change resulted in universal male suffrage with nomination of the president being made in conventions rather than by Congress and state legislatures.

If revolution is understood in the context of liberation, a struggle for national independence may or may not be

6. Leon Whipple, *The Story of Civil Liberty in the United States* (New York: Vanguard Press, Inc., 1927), p. 10.

revolutionary. It must be judged by its impact. The more superficial the change in values and institutions, the less revolutionary. In the case of the American War of Independence there were some changes made that could not be said to be simply acceptance of the British pattern. But the aim of freedom from the kind of centralized policies and control symbolized by the British crown was nullified by the adoption of the Constitution and by other policies similar to those formerly used by England. Over the long term it is apparent that the president of the United States has been able to exercise more power, in spite of built-in checks and balances, than did George III or his successors, including the king's prime ministers.

Frequently the term *revolution* has been applied to struggles for national independence simply because of the popular identification of substantial violence with revolution to which we alluded earlier. The achievement of Canadian or Australian independence without war has not been called revolutionary. The reason, however, should not be the absence of violence but the fact that these independent Commonwealth nations maintained essentially the same political and economic system as before independence. India on the other hand can more properly be said to have been freed by a revolution under Gandhi's leadership, for two reasons: (1) freedom of India started a chain reaction that led to the ending of colonialism and thus established a different relationship between former Asian and African colonies and the rest of the world; and (2) Gandhi demonstrated, on a larger scale than had ever been tried before, the use of a completely new method of achieving independence—massive noncooperation, or nonviolent resistance. India, however, did not move to a new economic or political system which gave real power to the people. Its failure to move in this direction was not a result of its revolutionary method of nonviolence, for Nehru and other Congress party leaders were not committed to nonviolence but to following Gandhi's leadership. Subsequently India, under Nehru, built an army, invaded and conquered Goa and fought Pakistan over Kashmir. The partial success of nonviolent struggle for independence, as Theodor Ebert observed, "did create the political climate in which a social revolution could be achieved by a second non violent insurrection, if not by parliamentary means."[7]

The fact that some nations have won their independence without violence and some have eliminated oppressive regimes without violence has not been sufficient to destroy the popular stereotype that revolutions must necessarily be violent. Within recent years a cult of violence has grown around the idea that the only real power is violence. Mao Tse-tung has phrased it for many who believe in revolutionary change, by saying that "power grows out of the barrel of a gun." In this respect he differs from Marx who did not believe violence was the decisive factor in revolution. Marx and Engels believed that the contradictions in and the decadence of the old systems were responsible for their own destruction. Engels suggested that "whenever the power structure of a country contradicts its economic development, it is the political power and its use of violence that will suffer defeat."[8]

Violence is the same whether used by revolutionaries or counterrevolutionaries. There is no greater power in a liberator's gun than in an oppressor's. Violence in itself conveys no impression of goodness or rightness and hence of moral power. Those who use violence against entrenched systems of violence must have something more to support their position than weapons. If violence equals power then the government with superior violence is bound to win. Mao did not of course believe that superior violence equals

7. Theodor Ebert, "Non Violent Insurrection or Revolutionary Warfare," *Fellowship*, September 1968, p. 17.

8. Friedrich Engels in Herrn Eugen Dührings, *Umwälzung der Wissenschaft (1878)*, part II, chap. 4. As quoted in Hannah Arendt, *On Violence* (New York: Harcourt Brace & World, Inc., 1969), p. 9.

power because he twice challenged superior weaponry: in the war against Chiang Kai-shek and also in the Korean War against the United States. This means that he believed that something more than guns was needed for power, such as organization, strategy, morale, etc.

There is a more fundamental problem in Mao's statement which relates to the structure of government or of any political group. It is easy to assume that government rules by violence or by the threat of violence since the police and the army exist for the purpose of implementing governmental decisions by armed force or a display of force. The government's ability to use such armed force, however, depends on its ability to maintain the support of the people, including the police and the army. If they refuse to obey, violence is not power. In other words the power of government or of the leaders of any other social unit, including a group planning revolution, depends on the ability of those who lead or govern to win or maintain the cooperation and obedience of the people. There must always be the consent of the governed. Gandhi put it this way: "At the back of the policy of terrorism is the assumption that terrorism if applied in a sufficient measure will produce the desired result, namely bend the adversary to the tyrant's will. But supposing a people make up their mind that they will never do the tyrant's will?"[9]

If the power of any political unit is dependent on the cooperation and consent of those to whom guns have been given, the real power doesn't grow out of the barrel of a gun but out of the ability to influence or control those who have the guns. This means that power lies at a more basic level than the barrel of a gun. Robert MacIver points out that "force alone never holds a group together. A group may dominate by force the rest of the community but the initial group already subject to government before it can

9. Mohandas Gandhi, *Non-violence in Peace and War* (Ahmedabad: Navajivan Publishing House, 1942–62), vol. 1, p. 185.

dominate, is not cemented by force."[10] The cement for all social groups is a common interest or a common enemy. The power of the group depends on its cooperation or solidarity, "its organizing ability, its leadership, its resources and its resourcefulness, its tenacity of purpose and other things."[11]

Power, then, is the ability to accomplish purpose. The word itself is derived from the Latin verb *posse* and the French *pouvoir* which mean "to be able."

When a large nation is spoken of as a "great power" the reference is to the collective ability of its people to use their resources to accomplish purpose. The fact that large nations also have strong armed forces is what superficially suggests that power is identical with the ability to use violence. The further fact that large armies and air forces with effective firepower have been overpowered by small armies with no air power as evident in Vietnam is significant. There a relatively small Vietnamese force defeated the French and subsequently nullified the even stronger United States armed forces. More significant, however, is the fact that India, Ghana, Zambia, and other countries used nonviolent power to win their independence from the well-armed British. The French, the British, and the Americans while theoretically more powerful could not command the united support of their people whereas their "weaker" opponents had more solidarity, tenacity of purpose, and greater morale.

Hannah Arendt views power as action in concert or arising out of cooperation. "When we say of somebody that he is 'in power' we actually refer to his being empowered by a certain number of people to act in their name." So she adds that "the extreme form of power is All against One. . . ."[12] Neither government nor any political group

10. Robert MacIver, *The Web of Government* (New York: Macmillan, 1947), p. 16.
11. Ibid.
12. Arendt, *On Violence*, pp. 42, 44.

that would displace it can exist without power based on people who cooperate or have solidarity. Violence is not the essence of power but the instrument of power. It is almost identical with weapons. Violence like all instruments in the hands of people must be justified by some purpose which those people accept and must be guided or directed with some proportion. Otherwise it will destroy the purpose for which it was used and possibly those who use it. That is the reason that thermonuclear weapons cannot be used in any numbers. Their use will destroy, through radioactive fallout, not only the enemy but the people they were designed to defend.

If violence does not equal power but is by nature a tool of power it follows that violence is not effective if the power on which it is based disintegrates. The ultimate form of power is not violence but the solidarity of people committed tenaciously to a common purpose.

The insistence by Mao or anyone else that violence is the best way to accomplish a revolutionary purpose has another built-in defect. The gun symbolizes an attitude toward persons—that they are expendable if they stand in your way. Jacques Ellul wrote:

Once you start using violence, you cannot get away from it. Violence expresses the habit of simplification of situations, political, social or human. And a habit cannot quickly be broken. . . . It simplifies relations with the other completely by denying that the other exists. And once you have repudiated the other, you cannot adopt a new attitude—cannot, for example, start rational dialogue with him.[13]

Governments or administrations that simplify their relations with people by emphasizing that they will get what they want by violence are in the process of alienating the people on whom their power depends.

The power of government is not broken by violence but

13. Jacques Ellul, *Violence.* (New York: The Seabury Press, Inc., 1969), p. 94.

by collapse or decay—when the people, including the police and the army, or a substantial part of the people, are
no longer prepared to support the government with their
obedience or consent. So long as the bulk of the people
obey or support their government, state power is superior
to the weapons a minority can bring to bear.

In turn, this means that there can be no revolution without a revolutionary situation. A revolutionary situation can
be said to exist when an economic, political, social, or
military system is so insufferable that masses of people
have in their hearts withdrawn consent from the system or
from those who govern or manage it. This means that the
alienation of the people by a government or by the administrators of a system is more basic to a revolutionary situation than poverty or any other deprivation. People do put
up with poverty or other oppressive social conditions when
these seem necessary or inevitable. But when people realize
that their poverty or suffering is not necessary, that they
are simply objects of exploitation and that government
leaders don't really care about them, they no longer feel
that they are partners or even silent supporters of the government; they withdraw consent. Such withdrawal of consent does not usually begin with the very poor or with
underprivileged minorities. It often begins with the alienation of intellectuals from the system and with their sympathy toward those who suffer the most. The intellectuals in
turn do the agitation and make the mass of underprivileged
people aware of their plight, of the role of the system, and
of ways of dealing with it.

When there is a withdrawal of consent within the ranks
of those who administer the system there is also a weakness
or deterioration that takes place which robs the system of
vitality and efficiency and thus makes it more vulnerable to
opposition. Louis Gottschalk points out that

. . . unrest alone is insufficient to create a revolution. . . . there
must exist a sense of solidarity among the restless; and they

must also have leadership and some program of reform. Even with all these . . . revolutions have been known to fail if they met with effective conservative resistance; and hence it follows that revolutions succeed not so much because the revolutionaries are strong as because the vested interests are weak—or, to use Hegelian terms, not so much because antithesis is irresistible as because thesis has collapsed.[14]

Revolutions, then, grow out of the weakness of the systems or the government rather than out of the capacity of the revolutionaries for armed struggle. In other words *revolutions grow out of the disintegration of consent, not out of violence*. The reason violence is so often associated with revolution is that few have tested the power of government or the consent of the governed—except those who in their anger and frustration have been prepared to use violence. The disintegration of consent is generally the result of the suffering and indignities imposed upon people by the structures of violence which are a part of the established order. In addition to a revolutionary situation there must be some significant leadership or group action against the established order which provides an alternative to that establishment. In other words, withdrawal of consent can only be made manifest by a confrontation with the government of sufficient duration that the people demonstrate their support of the new option and their disobedience to or withdrawal of support from the old order. The new option necessarily must seem realizable and hopeful in its appeal. Without hope or the appeal of the future there would be no dynamic great enough to inspire revolutionary commitment.

The confrontation or group defiance of the established authority need not be violent. It can be nonviolent, as evident in such colonial revolts as in India, Zambia, and

14. Louis Gottschalk, "The Place of the American Revolution in the Causal Patterns of the French Revolution" in Herman Ausubel, ed., *The Making of Modern Europe* (New York: Dryden Press, 1951), p. 501.

Ghana; or it can be violent, as in Algeria or Cuba. Since all governments and systems exist only with the consent of the people, the problem those desiring revolution must face is whether to demonstrate the withdrawal of consent by violent or nonviolent methods.

A brief examination of two revolutions in Latin America will illustrate how central to each was the withdrawal of consent. The first of these, the Cuban Revolution (treated in more detail in chapter six), used violence as a method of confrontation. Batista, who was a former army sergeant, ruled Cuba with the aid of the army and the support of the United States. He allied himself with organized labor and had done various favors for labor leaders. He even had a prominent Communist in his cabinet. However, many educated and middle-class citizens had never accepted the coup of 1952 that brought Batista to power for the second time. In addition he enriched himself and continued his earlier practice of giving the armed forces a share in the national revenues.

Consent was really withdrawn by the middle class from Batista's dictatorship after the 1952 coup. But in 1955 came the first serious challenge to his regime in the form of student disturbances. These were followed by army conspiracies and then in December 1956 by an invasion of some eighty men under the leadership of Fidel Castro, only a dozen of whom survived. These went into the mountains and began to organize for guerrilla warfare. "The years 1957 and 1958," wrote Edwin Lieuwen, "were marked by further Army restlessness, a nearly successful naval revolt, and an expansion of Castro's guerrilla operations. Urban labor backed the dictator [Batista] . . . while the middle groups and the peasantry hoped to bring him down and restore constitutional government."[15]

By 1958 Castro had made it "unsafe for buses and trains

15. Edwin Lieuwen, *Arms and Politics in Latin America* (New York: Praeger, 1960), p. 100.

to operate on schedule in many parts of Cuba because of armed attacks. Tourists almost stopped going to Cuba."[16] Castro's followers kidnapped American business and military men and then released them, thus capturing the imagination of many Cubans. He succeeded in winning first the rural population, then the business and professional groups and only later the urban workers. When Castro's small bands left the Sierra Maestra to enter other parts of Cuba, Batista sent an army to destroy them. "His army swarmed into the affected areas only to surrender or melt away."[17]

Lieuwen summarized the Castro victory in these words:

The regular army, in the face of mass antagonism toward the regime and repeated guerrilla successes began losing its will to fight. Air force pilots began to desert rather than follow out orders to bomb defenseless cities. Faced with the distasteful prospect of having to conduct wholesale slaughter in an attempt to quell the swelling popular opposition, the army generals went to Batista and forced his resignation.[18]

On January 1, 1959, Batista fled Cuba and on January 2 Che Guevera took over Havana with only six hundred men. Professor Fagg wrote:

The Batista regime had lost the respect of the people and had collapsed. Castro's guerrilla forces had not bested the soldiers in the field nor had crowds in the cities overpowered the authorities. Economic conditions had not driven a maddened population to revolt; on the contrary, they had been rather good, and many of Castro's most ardent followers were well-to-do. Psychological factors mainly explain the triumph of the revolution.[19]

The Castro success is explained by the withdrawal of consent from Batista's regime and by a relatively small-scale violent confrontation which lasted long enough to

16. John Edwin Fagg, *Cuba, Haiti and the Dominican Republic* (Englewood Cliffs, N.J.: Prentice-Hall, Inc., 1965), p. 97.
17. Ibid., p. 98.
18. Lieuwen, *Arms and Politics*, p. 100.
19. Fagg, *Cuba, Haiti*, p. 98.

convince the army that the people were opposed to Batista.

The second or Guatemalan Revolution also involved withdrawal of consent and a confrontation with the government. The confrontation, however, was nonviolent even in the face of government violence. Guatemala was ruled by a brutal dictator, General Jorge Ubico, from March 15, 1931 to July 1, 1944. Ubico was referred to as "the Napoleon of the Tropics." He had ruled with the support of the United States and in the interests of the United Fruit company and other rich landowners. *Time* magazine reported a massacre which took place three years after Ubico became president of Guatemala:

> . . . scores of students, workers, prominent citizens suspected of plotting a rebellion were seized in their homes, killed without formality. Hundreds were thrown into prison, tortured, executed. Cried Ubico, admirer of Hitler's 1934 bloodpurge, "I am like Hitler, I execute first and give trial afterwards. . . ."[20]

Ubico was so tyrannical and unjust that the people of Guatemala had, in their hearts, withdrawn consent from his government. But no one seemed ready to challenge Ubico until the Atlantic Charter, drawn up by Franklin Roosevelt and Winston Churchill, was published. That charter to which Ubico nominally subscribed as an ally of the United States declared that every nation had a right to choose its own form of government. Forty-five Guatemalan lawyers decided to use the charter as a basis for petitioning Ubico to remove a judge who had handled most of the political trials and had invariably jailed those opposing Ubico's rule. A newspaper published their charges against the judge. This led to a series of events, including a manifesto announcing the formation of a new political party; a petition by two hundred schoolteachers for a wage increase, followed by their dismissal; and a petition by university students which included seven demands be-

20. *Time*, 26 June 1944, p. 45.

ginning with autonomy for the university. The students threatened a strike if the demands were not met.

Ubico declared a state of emergency with every citizen subject to immediate arrest. The manifesto about a political party, which had not been made public, was dropped and 311 prominent Guatemalans instead signed a manifesto asking Ubico to resign. He had once said that if three hundred honorable and respected Guatemalans would ask him to resign he would do so. Two lawyers entered the palace, presented the manifesto to the president's secretary, and managed to leave. About the same time university students marched past the U.S. embassy in a public demonstration only a day after all the schools had closed because of a teachers' strike.

Later in the evening hoodlums, encouraged by the police, attacked people in a lower-class area who were celebrating a religious feast in the open air. The police joined the attack, causing many injuries and imprisoning hundreds. The next day hundreds of women dressed in mourning clothes formed a street procession after meeting in the Church of San Francisco. Armed cavalry charged the women, killing one teacher and wounding many others. "Guatemala responded with a general strike. The streets were deserted. Only the sinister footsteps of the dictator's guards resounded. Stores, theaters, banks, schools, clinics, offices—all were closed. The city was a cemetery . . ."[21]

Ubico tried to intimidate and then negotiate with the 311 prominent citizens. The U.S. ambassador, Boas Long, tried to save Guatemala for Ubico but the Mexican and some other diplomatic representatives defended the people who wanted Ubico to go.[22]

The *Time* account of July 10, 1944, is concise and descriptive:

21. Marie Rosenthal, *Guatemala: The Story of an Emergent Latin American Democracy* (New York: Twayne Publishers, Inc., 1962), pp. 202–10.
22. Ibid., p. 212, 213.

An unarmed national strike drove President Jorge Ubico, Tyrant of Guatemala, from office last week.

Students began the movement, but it quickly spread through the population. Shopkeepers closed their doors. Railroad workers quit. The people used little or no violence, for this was a strike of "brazos caidos" (arms down). The life of long-terrorized Guatemala slowed to a deathly standstill.

Ubico used plenty of violence. His police and soldiers ranged the capital, threatening, killing. But the strike did not lose force. Day by day like a fangless constrictor it tightened its coils around the encircled tyrant.

After a week or so, the tyrant yielded slightly and fired his strongest supporter, General David H. Ordonez, head of his Gestapo. The people were not appeased; they were after Ubico himself. At last after twelve days he handed his resignation to Congress, begged that his person and wealth be spared, set out for the frontier.

Before leaving Guatemala for Mexico City Ubico delegated his power to a military junta. But the people wanted real self-government.

There was an attempt made by one of the military junta, General Federico Ponce Vaides, to succeed Ubico as the strong man or political boss. This caused a popular uprising which included students, teachers, workers, and a group of young army officers, who carried out a military coup which ousted him on October 20, 1944. Then university students and boy scouts policed Guatemala City while the people voted. They elected Dr. Juan José Arevalo, a university professor, as President. Thereafter, until the United States Central Intelligence Agency intervened, Guatemala adopted and functioned under a liberal constitution which granted rights to labor, prohibited any discrimination because of sex, race, color, class, religious beliefs, or political ideas. It even guaranteed the right of the people to rebel if the president violated the rule against succeeding himself in office.

The experience of both Cuba and Guatemala suggests that a powerless government which is powerless precisely because it has lost popular support, is defeated by persistent confrontation, whether violent or nonviolent. But this raises an important ethical question. If it is possible either by violence or nonviolence to bring a government down, why should violence be used? Or, put another way, why should revolutionary groups plan for maximum violence when either no violence or minimal violence will be at least as effective?

There are of course some possible answers to this. One of these is that attempted revolutions are more often the product of anger than rational planning, and anger seeks to hurt or kill the adversary. But this is an explanation rather than a justifiable reason, given the fact that revolutionaries, unless they are nihilists, have an interest in a better society after the revolution.

A second possible explanation of the use of violence is that men psychologically tend to believe there is something more virile or manly about inflicting blows than absorbing them. Yet a more careful analysis reveals that there is nothing courageous about a shot in the dark, a kidnapping, or hit-and-run guerrilla raids in which the violence is directed at others. Violence is more an aspect of cowardice than of courage since it seeks to avoid personal suffering while inflicting it on others. Courage is involved only when men themselves run risks of death or injury. In this respect those who, like Gandhi's followers, stood up to and absorbed the blows of the British soldiers, or like Martin Luther King's black men, women and children, marched unarmed toward brutalized southern police and Klansmen, were obviously people of courage.

A third possible explanation is ignorance of the political process or of nonviolence. There are, for example, both North and South Americans whose only knowledge of nonviolence has come from news reports of demonstrations by black people in some southern parts of the United States. They assume that this is the essence of nonviolence and doubt if it could work in their situation. Or they rec-

ognize the power of a labor strike but do not have control
of one or more unions. They fail to see the power of a
consumer boycott. Or they believe it is easier to organize a
little band of guerrillas than to organize an effective boycott.

Still another reason for the tendency of revolutionaries
to prefer violence is that they doubt a revolutionary situation exists. They either believe they are only a small minority without popular support or they doubt that the government has created an obviously intolerable situation. Their
use of violence prior to the existence of a genuinely revolutionary situation is intended to provoke the government or
make it overreact so that it restricts the liberties of the
people even further. Under these circumstances such violence is intended to make the people believe that the existing government cannot preserve order except by becoming
so brutal and tyrannical as no longer to merit popular
support. This raises at least two problems. One is whether a
minority that can win only by such terrorism will not also
terrorize the people once it achieves power. Instead of
being the instrument of a people who need liberation it has
decided to create the conditions that will justify liberation.
The Marxist analysis, contrary to this, held that it was not
possible by violence to create a genuinely revolutionary
situation. That situation unfolded or developed as a result
of its own internal contradictions. Marx believed that in a
revolutionary situation violence was the midwife of revolution. He did not assume that violence created or conceived
the child or nourished it during pregnancy. In fact he
recognized the possibility that revolutionary change could
occur without violence.

The second problem in the tendency of minorities to use
violence is their failure or refusal to explore alternative
methods to test the government or mobilize the people. If
the government is in fact unwilling or unable to meet the
needs and aspirations of the people, this can be demonstrated by strikes, boycotts, land invasions, sit-ins, or other

forms of nonviolence. If the government overreacts to essentially peaceful demands for change, governmental tyranny becomes evident quite as much as if violence were used. But the government or power structure is then uniquely responsible for the violence. If the people cannot be organized either clandestinely or openly even in a relatively passive boycott, it is obvious that the people have not yet been the butt of intolerable injustice. Nonviolent methods require the participation of the people and therefore are evidence of at least a prerevolutionary dissatisfaction. Violence on the other hand does not in itself demonstrate anything except the anger of those able to acquire and use weapons.

Sometimes it is argued that a totalitarian or ruthless regime will not permit nonviolent opposition. This implies that nonviolent resistance to a regime is carried on only with the consent or collaboration of the government. The fact that democratic governments may permit nonviolent protest does not mean that such protest is possible only with such permission. It is difficult both for violent and nonviolent groups to organize their opposition to a totalitarian government. In neither case does the regime permit opposition. The reason some revolutionaries believe it is easier to be violent is due to their assumption that nonviolence involves overt demonstrations that can be easily crushed. A boycott, however, is not easily stopped. How, for example, can any regime force people to buy and use a particular product? The organization of a selective boycott can be clandestinely done if there is popular opposition to government that is kept covert only by the use of police and military terror. How can the government force people to go to church or the theater or otherwise participate in the usual cultural life of the nation? These are reverse demonstrations that can help build a revolutionary situation.

One of the most potent reasons for violent revolution is what Bart de Ligt calls "the orthodoxy of violence." By this he means that so many conflicts throughout history have been violent and history books, novels, and tradition have glorified or romanticized it as the way to deal with injustice or oppression, that it has become a way of life. This faith in violence is aided by the users of violence such as Hitler, Stalin, Mao, Castro, Churchill, and United States leaders who try to justify their use of violence in moral terms. It has been aided also by theologians who see violence as the only way to deal with powerful enemies. Violence is orthodox in the sense that it has become a kind of god by which some men live and to which other men turn as a matter of last resort. Many persons who claim faith in a god of love really view love as a distant ideal with little relevance to difficult contemporary problems. They hold that violence is a more effective way of dealing with issues.

Jacques Ellul expresses this differently:

> Christians who participate in violence are generally of a distressingly simplistic cast of mind. Invariably they judge socio-political problems on the basis of stereotyped formulas which take no account of reality. . . . They do not even stop to consider that when the violence is over, few if any problems will have been resolved and the real problems will arise.[23]

Perhaps even more fundamental than tradition or simplistic analysis is anger or hatred as a motivation for violence. When people endure a great deal of oppression and have no evidence of any compassion on the part of those associated with administering the systems that hold them down, it is understandable that they should hate those who are wealthy or powerful or otherwise benefit from the system. Hatred and anger drive people to seek revenge or to destroy their opponents in the process of seeking power themselves. But hatred and anger as bases for revolution can only destroy. They are not a motivation for a constructive program nor for eventual reconciliation with either

23. Jacques Elull, *Violence* (New York: The Seabury Press, Inc., 1969), pp. 60, 61.

victorious or defeated enemies. There is a certain nihilism about hatred which sanctions destruction for its own sake, whether it leads to anything creative or not. This was expressed in a statement by some students in Puerto Rico in December 1969. They were frustrated by a university administrator who had cancelled a meeting at which they had scheduled this writer to speak. In reaction they talked of burning a university building in spite of having no purpose they thought they could achieve. Hatred and anger tend to be nihilistic precisely because they have no purpose beyond destruction of the existing system.

Nevertheless violent revolutionary movements directed at freedom from colonial or other rule do exist and must be understood. It is not helpful to condemn such movements especially if there is no nonviolent movement of liberation, for the alternative is support of colonial or other violent structures. Revolutionary movements engage in violence generally because their leaders are not convinced that other or better methods are available. In unindustrialized societies, such as those under Portuguese rule, a boycott or strike may have little effect. It would be presumptuous for white Americans who have never lived in Angola or Mozambique to prescribe a course of revolutionary action there. On the other hand, other African peoples in nonindustrial states have secured their freedom without armed revolution. Industrial societies such as the Republic of South Africa which are dependent on black labor are vulnerable to strikes, boycotts, and mass emigration.

At the end of 1971 about thirteen thousand Ovambos of South West Africa, about a third of the labor force in the territory administered by South Africa, left their "jobs in the white-run mining, fishing and industrial enterprises . . . and returned to their tribal homeland in the north." They did not agree to return to work until the system was ended that restricted them to long periods of work with one employer and also limited their earning power. They won the right to change jobs, to have shorter contracts, paid leave, higher pay, and freedom "to negotiate directly with employers instead of through an official recruiting organization."[24]

Some people, however, continue to view violence as the decisive factor in human affairs. This is implied in such ideas as nonviolence could work only against a humane nation or in a free society but not in the overwhelming number of situations where there are tough adversaries. This of course overlooks the fact that the British army and air force in India were tough and ruthless and that nonviolent action against racial segregation in the United States was more successful in Alabama and Mississippi than in less feudal parts of the nation. Ultimately the question of violence as an article of faith will be determined by a rational examination of its results. If it does not produce genuine liberation but instead ends in oppression, faith in violence has been misplaced. Faith in violence necessarily means that the universe is so organized that it is friendly to superior violence or to lesser violence wielded with greater moral purpose. It implies that freedom and equality are more likely to be won by harming or destroying others and hence by a process contrary to freedom and equality.

The use of violence whether as defense of law and order or as revolution is not a struggle for equality but for superiority; it is not a struggle to exalt personality by respecting it, but an effort to destroy or degrade those who are the class or racial or national enemies. Violence by its very nature seeks to make persons unequal by incapacitating them so that they cannot express themselves as freely or fully as those who are using violence against them. Often, as in war, violent revolution makes them permanently unequal through death or serious injury.

There are objections to nonviolent revolution just as there are objections to violent revolution. Among these are the difficulty of mobilizing large groups of people, of main-

24. *New York Times*, 1 February 1972.

taining a nonviolent discipline in the face of provocation and of continuing group solidarity and discipline after the reins of power have been seized. In India, and some other countries that won their independence by nonviolent struggle, new leaders or old ones abandoned any effort to continue nonviolent change based on decentralizing of political and economic control.

Basically the problem for every revolution is what is the most appropriate power for the ending of oppression and the creation of a new and liberating order. An examination of modern revolutions or attempts at revolution may be helpful in determining their weaknesses and strengths. In evaluating these revolutions it must be remembered that the results of revolution are not static. One of the crucial questions underlying all of the others is to what extent societies remain creatures of their past. Widespread revolutionary violence may be a conditioning agent that cheapens human life not only in the course of the struggle but in its immediate aftermath. Yet this thwarting of the revolutionary purpose must not be an occasion for a simplistic indictment of revolution. Rather it should be an incentive for finding new ways to make the revolutionary vision concrete.

5

THE IMPACT OF VIOLENCE
ON REVOLUTION

The contemporary world contains a number of nations whose governments were born in revolution. It is frequently assumed that these revolutions began and ended in armed violence simply because the seizure of power was violent. In actuality the typical revolution began long before the seizure of power and continued for years or decades following that seizure.

The Chinese Revolution, for example, was not confined to the conflict between the Communists led by Mao Tse-tung and the Kuomintang led by Chiang Kai-shek. Rather it could be said to have begun either with the breakup of the imperial rule and the establishment of the republic in 1911 or with the Taiping Rebellion (1850–1865) which set in motion ideas and processes that foreshadowed the Communist movement. As a result, when the Communists came to power in China they found that their predecessors had broken through some of the greatest social barriers to communism and had paved the way with a vision of new social and national relationships.

Revolutions begin when people dream of something better than what they have. They withdraw their consent to or support of the established order when they identify it as oppressive or experience the structural violence by which it maintains itself. Both events and propaganda contribute to the exposure of such violence and the delegitimizing of the system. Generally there is a vanguard or revolutionary elite which organizes those who are alienated from the system and thus spearheads the development of a party or mass movement. Its purpose is to overthrow the political system rather than to modify it by becoming the leaders of that system. Because it assumes that the seizure of power must be accomplished by violence, the revolutionary elite tends to adopt a conspiratorial and military approach to organization, with a leader, secret disciplined cells, and an authoritarian type of organization. This military approach in the founding organization generally, if not always, has a carry-over into the political organization of the new regime. This is one of the reasons that so many revolutionary governments are authoritarian or totalitarian in the decades following the seizure of power.

There are, of course, other reasons for revolutionary dictatorships and ruling elites such as the fear to relinquish armed controls because of rival or counterrevolutionary elements that will wipe out what has been achieved. Such motives are often mixed with the human desire to maintain or increase power over people once it has been experienced.

However, something more than the continuation in power of the revolutionary party is evident in any true revolution. The oppressive systems inherited from the old order must be replaced or transformed into new and liberating structures. There must also be a continuing improvement of the welfare of the people so that they move not only toward a better physical life but toward controlling their own destinies. This means that the ruling elite must encourage structures which could pass out of their control. A revolutionary party which sets up static forms designed to perpetuate rule by a small elite or class soon ceases to be revolutionary.

If the essence of a genuine revolution is liberation, there should be decentralization of power so that the people themselves share in decision making. There should also be an end to special privilege, to armies and secret police, to imperialism or threats to other countries. In short, liberation requires social peace as well as participatory democracy.

Most of the modern revolutionary movements in one form of words or another originally identified themselves with the above goals. In each of the major modern revolutionary nations, armed violence was used to take control of the government. In each of them there were serious problems following the use of armed conquest that seemed to stand in the way of the revolution. In considering the impact of violence on revolution or whether violence is counterproductive, a number of questions will be considered: To what extent has violent conquest resulted in (1) a power struggle among the revolutionary leaders for dominance; (2) centralization of power in the army and/or bureaucracy; (3) a real or imagined threat to other countries which react with varying degrees of hostility; (4) serious damage to the economy of the nation undergoing revolution; and (5) continuing oppression or failure to democratize?

POWER STRUGGLES

In each of the major revolutionary movements there has been a power struggle among either factions or persons that were prominent in the revolution. Such a power struggle is usually the result of ideological or procedural differences, although personal ambition often plays a part. In the case of the Russian Revolution the struggle began after the tenth party congress in 1921 when the secret police began to suppress opposition elements within the party.

The Politburo decided that every party member had a duty to denounce all other members of the party who engaged in opposition activity or agitation against party leaders.[1]

During the revolution and the first few years that the Communist party (Bolsheviks) was in power, Lenin was its dominating figure. When he died in 1924 the struggle at the top began. The six men who had ruled Russia following the first seizure of power were Lenin, Trotsky, Zinoviev, Kamenev, Bukharin, and Stalin (after Sverdlov's death). Stalin, who had succeeded Sverdlov as the key person in charge of the work of the secretariat of the Central Committee, was in a position to appoint subordinate secretaries, to select delegates to party congresses and to control the Cheka or secret police. The secretariat was the commission for official promotions. In addition to using this machinery, Stalin allied himself with Kamenev and Zinoviev against Trostky who, all assumed, was the most likely successor to Lenin. Stalin also pitted Bukharin against Trotsky. In this way Stalin was able to checkmate or defeat Trotsky on every important committee. In January 1925 Trotsky was forced to give up his position as war commissar and chairman of the Revolutionary Military Committee. By the time it became apparent that Stalin would emerge as the successor to Lenin it was too late. With Trotsky's influence curtailed, it was impossible for Kamenev, Zinoviev, and Trotsky to prevail against Stalin at the fourteenth party congress (December 1925). By the end of 1926 all three had been expelled from the Politburo and in 1927 expelled from the party. Trotsky was also expelled from the Soviet Union in 1929 and assassinated in Mexico City in 1940. He had continued his opposition to Stalin outside the USSR.

Stalin also moved against Bukharin who was secretary of the committee and editor of *Izvestiia*, against Tomsky, the

---

1. Robert Conquest, *The Great Terror: Stalin's Purge of the Thirties* (New York: Macmillan, 1968), p. 6.

head of the Council of Trade Unions and Rykov the chairman of the Supreme Economic Council. These three, known as oppositionists of the Right, had opposed the expulsion of non-Stalinists from the Politburo and were also opposed to the centralization of all party power in the hands of Stalin. The three men were expelled from the Politburo. Stalin, as he rose to the pinnacle of power, eliminated and killed the leaders of the revolution, just as Robespierre did. Trotsky, Kamenev, Zinoviev, Bukharin, Rykov, and Tomsky were all destroyed by Stalin. Stalin arranged the assassination of Sergei Kirov who controlled the Leningrad organization and maintained his independence from Stalin. The Kirov murder was followed by hundreds of arrests and political trials. These led to the death of millions and caused this period of about four years (December 1934 through 1938) to be known as the Great Purge or the Great Terror. "Kirov's death," wrote Robert Conquest in his monumental study, *The Great Terror*, "was the keystone of the entire edifice of terror and suffering by which Stalin secured his grip on the Soviet peoples."[2] Step by step, Stalin approved of lists of persons to be executed. The purge finally resulted in crushing the party as such so that it became completely the tool of Stalin.[3]

The power struggle in China began before the seizure of power in the efforts of Mao Tse-tung to become chairman of the Chinese Communist party (CCP). Mao was political commissar of the Chinese Red Army. In 1929 and 1930 Mao and two others were ordered by Li Li-san, the head of the CCP, to attack Changsha and Nanchang. They failed but Mao used the failures against Li Li-san, accusing him of being an adventurer and opportunist. "Many in Li's immediate circle were brutally executed by Mao . . ."[4] Mao also was a rival of other groups in the party.

2. Ibid., p. 44.
3. Ibid., pp. 236–75.
4. Chow Ching-wen, *Ten Years of Storm* (New York: Holt, Rinehart & Winston, Inc., 1960), p. 77.

To ensure his ascendance, Mao ruthlessly eliminated large numbers of rival officers and other opponents in the Red Army and the soviet area under his control. In retaliation Liu Teh, a political commissar of a battalion in the Twentieth Red Army, led an attack on Fut'ien and released a group of Communist leaders whom Mao had had arrested.[5]

In spite of Mao's various attempts to gain power, Wang Ming, with the backing of the Returned Student Clique (returned from Russia), succeeded Li Li-san as head of the CCP. Wang Ming's successor, also a member of the Returned Student Clique, was successfully challenged by Mao and forced to step down as chairman of the Politburo at a meeting of that body in 1935 during the "long march."

After the victory of the CCP in 1949 there were six regional military commands and administrations. Kao Kang had ruled over one of these even before the long march was made. Jao Shu-shih was the head of the East China region. These two men were purged about 1954 after being accused of using their strong regional position to gain power on the national level and all the regional bureaus were abolished. Kao Kang allegedly committed suicide and Jao was put in prison. Apparently Kao and Jao were seeking the positions held by Chou En-lai as premier of the State Council and Liu Shao-chi as vice-chairman of the Central Committee. Kao's rank in the CCP was just below Chou and Liu.

In the years immediately following the victory over Chiang Kai-shek, Mao's influence and control over the CCP was great. But following the "Great Leap Forward," which he pushed, his influence diminished. The Great Leap Forward was a crash program of industrialization and of the formation of rural or agricultural communes. It was the failure of this combined program that led to a lessening

5. Franklin W. Houn, *A Short History of Chinese Communism* (Englewood Cliffs, N.J.: Prentice-Hall, Inc., 1967), p. 42.

of Mao's influence. In December 1958 at a meeting of the CCP Central Committee Mao was asked to give up his position as president of the republic while continuing as chairman of the party. Liu Shao-chi was chosen as president by the National People's Congress in April 1959 and again in January 1965. Political power from 1959 to 1962 was for the most part held by President Liu, Chou En-lai, and Teng Hsiao-ping. They called a halt to the public criticism of the Soviet Union, gave intellectuals more freedom, and gave peasants and workers more incentives to increase production.

Mao used the idea of the danger of a return to capitalism as the basis for regaining power. He began in 1962 at a full meeting of the central committee to issue his warnings. Thereafter until the Great Proletarian Revolution of 1966–67,[6] Mao gradually stepped up his warnings and programs of education until he felt strong enough to launch a series of purges. The first purge was of the Peking party committee followed by the dismissal of the heads of five universities. Then Mao succeeded in having Marshal Lin Piao named in August 1966 as his successor instead of Liu who, prior to his election as president, was being prepared as Mao's successor. Before long Liu Shao-chi became the chief target of the Red Guards, organized by Mao among students to demonstrate against everything revisionist or bourgeois. The Red Guards attacked others who had supported Liu personally or ideologically against Mao. Peng Chen, the mayor of Peking and number nine in the Communist hierarchy, was arrested by Red Guards after they dragged him from bed one night during December 1966. "The Red Guards held daily rallies in a stadium for the denunciation of persons under attack" and those who were "criticized were frequently paraded through the streets in open lorries wearing paper dunces' caps two feet tall and

6. Also called Cultural Revolution.

placards round their necks giving details of the charges against them."[7]

There were also purges in the army of those who were not thoroughly loyal to Marshal Lin Piao, the new heir to Mao.[8] The purges and the Cultural Revolution did not end until the twelfth plenum of the Central Committee of the CCP, held in October 1968, had voted to dismiss Liu Shao-chi from all his government and party positions and to expel him from the party. The purges left only thirteen of the old Politburo, or fifty percent of its members, in good standing. Forty-eight of those in the Central Committee, or about fifty-one percent, were purged and "nine others severely criticized," leaving only thirty who were young enough to be active and in good standing. Of the first secretaries of provincial party committees, only five out of twenty-eight were still functioning.[9]

Not all of those purged were opponents of Mao. The fact that it took so long to eliminate President Liu indicated the strength Liu had within the party. The political upheaval evident in the Cultural Revolution "has taken an unprecedentedly large toll of party officials, Mao's foes and supporters alike, and has severely disrupted the party's machinery as well as undermined its authority and morale."[10] Mao was ultimately able to win as much as he did only by his alliance with Marshal Lin Piao and the People's Liberation Army (PLA). In order to win the struggle he finally had to settle for a Politburo with thirteen of the twenty-five full and alternate members wearing the PLA uniform. Four were district commanders in the army.

One difference in the Chinese power struggle of 1966–67

7. Keesing's Research Report, *The Cultural Revolution in China* (New York: Charles Scribner's Sons, 1967), pp. 6, 10, 11, 22–24.

8. Ibid., p. 25.

9. Parris H. Chang, "Mao's Great Purge: A Political Balance Sheet," *Problems of Communism*, March–April 1969, pp. 4, 6, 7.

10. Ibid., p. 4.

from that of the Russian is that few prominent persons lost their lives. Mao and his colleagues were either content with political victories and psychological humiliation of their opponents or else lacked the political strength to imprison or execute all the party leaders who had to be purged.

The purges of the Cultural Revolution, however, were not the end. Defense Minister Lin Piao has disappeared from the Chinese political ruling group and some other top ranking members of the armed forces have also been purged. Even more changes may be in the offing.

The power struggle pattern is not confined to Communist revolutions for it was evident also in Algeria after the fighting with the French had ended in March 1962 and independence was achieved. The first major conflict occurred when Youssef Ben Khedda, premier of the Provisional Government, then in Tunisia, dismissed the chief of the Algerian Army of National Liberation (ALN), Colonel Houari Boumedienne, and others on the general staff. Instead of accepting the dismissal, Boumedienne disappeared to avoid arrest or assassination and waited for his army units to rally around him. Meanwhile a conflict developed between Ben Khedda and his vice-premier, Ben Bella.

Ben Bella left Tunisia for Algiers where fighting had broken out between rival army units. There was fighting in the streets of the city as well as in the outskirts even after Ben Bella took power on August 7, 1962. The fighting was stopped in late August by the workers and civilians of Algiers who bodily put themselves between the fighting men. In early September Colonel Boumedienne, still the commander of the ALN, entered Algeria with seven thousand soldiers and made a declaration of allegiance to Ben Bella and the Political Bureau.

During Ben Bella's regime there were other power struggles. Ben Bella with the support of Boumedienne took over control from Mohammed Khider of the National Liberation Front which continued as a political party after independence. Khider wanted the party to have authority over the government. Ben Bella also arrested a former deputy premier of the Algerian Provisional Government and others whom he charged with plotting against the government. Ben Bella also tried to build up his own power as over against that of Boumedienne who had become first deputy premier. He promoted Colonel Tahar Zbiri to the post of chief of the general staff without consulting Boumedienne and tried to build up Colonel Chaabani of the Sahara Army unit in an effort to counter Boumedienne. Boumedienne captured Chaabani and his army and then had him executed.

Finally in June 1965 Colonel Boumedienne ended power struggles by a coup d'état in which he replaced and imprisoned Ben Bella. The Boumedienne coup was directed not only at Ben Bella but at the foreign and domestic advisers who were pushing Ben Bella to the Left. These were chiefly Russian, Chinese, Cuban, and United Arab Republic people.

A Turkish war correspondent who was pro-Algerian throughout the war against the French wrote: "It was this terrible rivalry more than the inherent complexities of the post-independence task that brought about the downfall of the revolution."[11]

Revolutionary power struggles are often implicit in the nature of the military type organization that seems necessary for the seizure of power. Those who accept the leader and the discipline necessary to overthrow a regime are not necessarily in accord with all the political and economic ideas that leader and some of his colleagues seek to implement. When there is no orderly way to appeal to the people and no orderly method for taking control of the revolutionary government, the result is often a power struggle within the revolutionary elite. Moreover the habit of con-

11. Arslan Humbaraci, *Algeria, A Revolution That Failed* (New York: Praeger, 1966), p. 5.

spiring and the use of armed force rather than open campaigning for control also enhance the probability of planned coups. Sometimes the power struggle occurs because of the illness or death of a dominant revolutionary figure; in another case it may be a leader's inadequate handling of a deteriorating economy or foreign affairs which moves some of his colleagues to displace him. In any event the desire on the part of some in the ruling group to get rid of others is often implemented by imprisonment, exile, or death. One reason is that the continued freedom of any revolutionary leader gives him the opportunity to build support for his cause. But since there is no orderly way for people to challenge those in command, any activity on his part against the decisions of the leadership is understood as mutiny.

CENTRALIZATION OF POWER

All of the major modern revolutionary movements function from a centralized power base in which the army or a party bureaucracy is dominant. In Algeria the army was the power behind the scenes during Ben Bella's regime but came out into the open when Colonel Boumedienne with the help of other officers took over the government. In 1963 when Ben Bella issued his unopposed list of candidates for election to the National Assembly there were seventy-two members, chiefly officers of the army. Ben Bella, however, wanted to do something to curb the army's power and established a people's militia in line with Che Guevara's advice to arm the people. Following the Boumedienne coup this militia was disbanded.

In the case of Russia the Communist party functions like an army as Lenin envisioned it. As early as 1903, during tsarist days, Lenin argued, at a congress of Russian social democrats meeting in London, that only those participating in the underground organization who were prepared to accept the discipline of a central leadership and act on its orders could be members of the Russian Social Democratic Worker's party. He envisioned the party as the instrument of revolution. He lost the decision but later organized the Bolshevik party whose Politburo planned the seizure of power in 1917.

The military structure and discipline of the Bolsheviks made it possiple for them to organize within the soviets which were councils of workers' and soldiers' deputies whose members were elected by workers in factories and soldiers in their barracks. The first soviets were elected by strikers in 1905. The strikes spread throughout the country after tsarist troops fired on a peaceful procession of workers who were marching to present a petition to the tsar. However, the soviets were forced to disband and the tsar remained in control. But in 1917, a few days before the tsar abdicated, the Petrograd soviet sprang into existence under Trotsky's leadership. The Petrograd soviet took control of that capital city in October 1917 and overthrew the provisional government. Prior to that the Bolsheviks were successful in getting the soviet to accept their program and to elect a Bolshevik majority in the soviet's Central Executive Committee. Following the takeover of the city and government an all-Russian congress of soviets took place which elected to its presidium a majority of Bolsheviks. Then came the successive conquest in November 1917 of a number of other Russian cities, including Moscow.

The original intent of the abortive Revolution of 1905 and of the majority of socialists in Russia was to have the country run by the soviets as representative, self-governing organizations or in other words as a decentralized republic run by producers' collectives. In practice every soviet organization was paralleled by a party organization which held a preliminary meeting to determine the proceedings of the soviet.

Long before Stalin became the real ruler of Russia the process of control from the top had begun, so that the Politburo controlled the soviets, the secret police, the army and the economy. All other political parties were abolished. Labor unions ceased to exist except as functions of the party hierarchy. No private organizations were permitted except for the churches.

The Red Army was created in January 1918 as a democratic and voluntary organization following the Treaty of Brest-Litovsk. Committees of soldiers actually elected their officers. Later in 1918 it was decided to move from a volunteer army to general conscription. When the armies were not fighting they were used as labor conscripts for industrial work. This led to conscription of labor as well. The Bolsheviks decreed that "all citizens . . . are subject to compulsory labor." Isaac Deutscher wrote that "the party that had promised to abolish the standing army was transforming the working population into an army."[12] Control over the army itself was exercised through members of the Communist party in the armed forces. They belonged to party branches at the various levels of command. There were also political commissars at the army command level and at regimental and company levels. Each military order was to be signed not only by the commander but also by the commissar. The commissar watched the officers and also was responsible for the political education of the troops.

Practically everything in the Soviet Union was centralized through a bureaucracy established and controlled by the party. Jules Monnerot described party control in these words:

The Party structure is vertical and business proceeds exclusively along vertical lines. Officials of the same rank in different departments are isolated from one another by water-tight compartments. Here the resemblance to an army is striking; at a given level men of the same rank and way of life have no means of combining against their official superiors. As Stalin himself

12. Isaac Deutscher, *Stalin: A Political Biography* (New York: Vintage Books, 1960), p. 219.

put it, the trade unions and soviets are simply "transmission belts" by which Party members can control the rest of the population in the same way that they themselves, within the Party are guided by a system of controls passing down by stages from the highest levels to the lowest.[13]

The Soviet Union also has its secret police. The Cheka which was created in 1917 was intended as an agency for uncovering any opponents of the regime. A secret political police of this sort is further evidence of "the uneasiness of the government at not being a product of peaceful evolution and at not being able to retain its position without violence . . ."[14]

What had begun as a revolution intended to end an absolute monarchy and provide a democratic socialism had been changed into a centralized and totalitarian tyranny. It was the Leninist assumption about violent seizure of power that led to the military type organization that characterizes the party and its bureaucracy to this day.

China, in its centralization of power in the army and the bureaucracy, clearly follows the pattern of other revolutions conditioned by the violent seizure of control of government. Following the seizure of power in 1949, the Chinese Communist party felt it essential to have a strong military establishment. This feeling was precipitated in part by the continued existence of the Chinese Nationalists, the Korean War, and the U.S. alliance with the Nationalists. But it was also an outgrowth of the victorious revolutionary army and the convictions of Mao that "power grows out of the barrel of a gun." The Chinese army was believed to be larger than any other, with about 2.3 million men in the postwar period. In addition China had a militia in 1950 of about five and a half million. In 1958 the CCP started a movement to make "Everyone a Soldier." It was a way to

13. Jules Monnerot, *Sociology of Communism* (London: George Allen and Unwin, Ltd., 1953), p. 75.
14. Ibid., p. 77.

militarize the people so that they could be indoctrinated by the militia organizations and also trained physically. Since the militia is intended to reinforce the People's Liberation Army and receives training at the hands of the PLA, there is thus a close relation of the people to the army. Mao also insisted that the army engage in economic production with soldiers joining civilians in farm and industrial work.

During the Cultural Revolution of 1966–67 Mao succeeded in having Marshal Lin Piao named as his successor. There were purges in the army of those who were not thoroughly loyal to Marshal Lin Piao. As indicated earlier other opponents of Mao were also purged. However, Mao was able to win as much as he did only by his alliance with Marshal Lin Piao and the PLA. The process by which Mao and Lin Piao used the army included placing various military personnel in political, governmental and educational institutions. Young "men recently 'retired' from the Army made their appearance in educational institutions. . . ." They "enrolled as students" and "later emerged as leaders of the student 'work groups' which established Red Guard units in educational institutions throughout the country."[15] Following the Cultural Revolution military influence in the CCP increased greatly. At least 58 of the 170 full members of the new Central Committee were "important military men."[16] Twenty-five members of the Politburo were in PLA uniforms. In addition "some 33 government ministries were headed by men transferred from the PLA."[17]

In 1971 Lin Piao and top ranking members of the armed forces in Peking were purged. There was also a campaign to downgrade the political role of the PLA. Nevertheless a survey made in early 1972 showed that "military figures

15. Franz Michael, "The Struggle for Power," *Problems of Communism*, May–June 1967, p. 19.

16. *New York Times*, 26 April 1969.

17. Stephen A. Sims, "The New Role of the Military," *Problems of Communism*, November–December 1969, pp. 26, 27.

still hold the concurrent positions of Communist party first secretary and chairman of the Revolutionary Committee in 17 of the 26 administrative units designated as either provinces or autonomous regions." Prominent party and administrative posts are held by military men in most other areas.[18]

Much less is known about the bureaucracy. It is obvious, however, that a nation the size of China which directed all economic, political, and social affairs and certain provincial committees from a central point requires an extensive and centralized bureaucracy. In 1950 when the government decided to increase production in agriculture it "issued a series of decrees outlining the structure of government at all levels of national life." This program "was accompanied by rapid bureaucratization" at all levels.[19]

The centralization of power in the Communist party, however, is the key to the whole question of centralization. The party's structure "stands alongside every unit of organization in the country. Factories, communes (and their production brigades), schools, government bureaus, military companies, and so on—all have their party committees. In turn these committees are composed of "most of the important leaders of the counterpart organizational unit."[20] Illustrations of the bureaucracy are seen in the Ministry of Finance which directs and regulates the Chinese economy, and the Ministry of Commerce which operates the extensive nationwide supply system.[21]

Mao Tse-tung is reported to be concerned about the growth of a tremendous bureaucracy in China. This is one of the reasons, joined with his own drive to vindicate his position, that led to the Cultural Revolution of 1966–67.

18. *New York Times*, 7 February 1972.
19. Franz Schurmann and Orville Schell, *Communist China, Revolutionary Reconstruction and International Confrontation 1949 to the Present* (New York: Random House, 1967), p. 173.
20. Ibid., p. 120.
21. Ibid., p. 138.

Mao saw the bureaucracy as primarily concerned with maintaining its own security and the status quo, thus being an instrument of conservatism. The results of his efforts, as we have observed, led to more army control of the nation. He tried to keep the army from being ruled by status quo generals by working out a system whereby high-ranking officers will serve for a month a year as ordinary soldiers at the company level and by conscription. Mao appears imbued with the liberal myth that conscription of civilians into the army civilizes the army rather than militarizes the population. In any event the fraternization of top officers with their soldiers has not eliminated the need for a military bureaucracy nor resulted in ordinary soldiers instead of top officers being put on the Politburo, the Central Committee, and provincial committees. On the other hand there is some evidence that the CCP intends to reassert the supremacy of the Central Committee over the military. The *New York Times* of February 7, 1972 reported a commentary in Peking's *Jenmin Jih Pao* which emphasized the party's constitutional directive: "The individual is subordinate to the organization, the minority is subordinate to the majority, the lower level is subordinate to the higher level and the entire party is subordinate to the Central Committee."

In the case of China, centralization of power may have been an asset in the early days of the revolution. Certainly the Communists have done what no other regime has done since the middle of the nineteenth century—unify the nation politically. But centralization of power in the form of a dictatorship that has increasingly become militarized is a by-product of an armed revolution, rather than the result simply of a need for political unity.

Centralization of power in a revolutionary party bureaucracy or in the army can be traced to essentially two factors: the organization of the party along military lines in order to seize power and the fear of counterrevolution after power has been gained. The military type organization of the party continues after it takes control of government because there is no reason to change a successful organization. It also continues because it is a highly disciplined organization controlled by a few men at the top who need the party machinery to manage the political and economic life of the nation.

The fear of counterrevolution is also rooted in the violent seizure of power. What one group can do presumably can be done by others. This fear was voiced by Kenneth Kuanda in 1963 before he became prime minister of Zambia. When he was asked why he did not use violence as the Algerians had in seeking their independence he replied:

> Even if we fought violently, and perhaps in a year or two managed to get what we wanted, we would have sown seeds of doubt in the country. Those who disagreed with us would have a precedent set for them, and they too would have to try to organize to overthrow us, or those who are then in power, through violent activities. History shows several times that the method you use in obtaining your objective is very often the method used by other people to try and throw you out of power.[22]

Certainly those who have used substantial violence for revolutionary purposes have feared the possibility of counterrevolutionary violence. The price paid for this fear is dictatorship or a high degree of centralized control of the people. Violence thus becomes a permanent part of the politics of staying in power, as is evident in the Soviet Union during the decades following the revolution.

The fear of counterrevolution makes it seem imperative not only to control the army and the police but any persons or organs that can sow dissension among the people or within the government itself. Totalitarianism is in effect the institutionalization of the revolutionary violence into a form of continued warfare against the people so that the

22. Theodor Ebert, "Nonviolent Insurrection or Revolutionary Warfare?" *Fellowship*, September 1968, p. 17.

ruling elite may not only stay in power but destroy and reconstruct social forces and systems at will. An iron rule becomes necessary when power is seized without the consent of the people or a significant portion of them. Those who do not consent or who appear reluctant to go along with the new regime are viewed as enemies or potential enemies to be excluded by the centralization of power.

Lawrence Stone indicates that "violence leads to bitter cleavages within the society which, as the French, English and American examples" suggest, "it may take between seventy and 150 years to weld together." He concludes that "the very use of violence creates a new situation demanding a new solution."[23]

The new situation of alienation ought to demand something other than continued violence, such as reconciliation with those who have been alienated in order to reestablish social peace. But revolutionary thinking based on violence increasingly views the enemy as someone to be subjugated or destroyed. This continual viewing as enemies those who did not consent to the armed seizure of power or those who in any way resist the new regime validates the centralized control over the people.

FOREIGN HOSTILITY

In almost every instance revolutions in one country have been seen by other nations as a threat. This may be because the example seems dangerous to the stability of their own ruling classes or because the revolutionaries are zealous in trying to export violent change. The revolution may also have expropriated the business investments of nationals of other countries, thus creating hostility.

In the case of Russia there was Allied intervention during World War I because the Allies wanted both to protect their supplies of arms stored in Russian ports and also to

23. *The New York Review of Books*, 24 August 1967, p. 34.

prevent the Germans from capitalizing on the Russian ending of hostilities along the entire eastern front. The French were concerned about their investments in Russia which had been nationalized by the Soviet government, while the Japanese had ambitions to build a territorial empire in eastern Siberia. In reaction to these interventions, the Communists appealed to workers in the Allied countries to stop the intervention. They also appealed to workers to revolt against their own governments. They believed that their own successful seizure of power was but the beginning of socialist revolutions that would sweep Europe.

The violence of the revolution, especially as it implied continuing efforts to start similar revolutions in other countires stimulated outside hostility. So also did the Communist and hence anticapitalist nature of the Russian Revolution. In time the Soviet Communist party alienated European and American socialists and many labor movements. The Russians were unwilling to tolerate any socialism that did not conform to the Russian model. The Communist International was not a committee drawn equally from other national traditions but a group bound to the defense and advancement of the Russian system. Party leaders in other countries had to function as army officers of the Communist party of the Soviet Union. A representative of the Comintern sat in party meetings in each country to insure no deviation from the Russian line. The result was the alienation of labor and socialist groups as well as business interests.

The Chinese Revolution resulted in a belief by other nations that China was a threat to their security. From a Chinese point of view the effort to stop American influence in or control of Korea, Japan, Taiwan, Vietnam, and Laos was an effort to end imperialism. From the United States perspective it was seen as a Chinese desire to control these nations. The Chinese military invasion of India in 1962, even though the Chinese subsequently withdrew, alienated India; the Communist party and some Chinese in Indonesia were seen by the Indonesian military as agents of the Chinese party. It is not necessary to describe the Chinese support of revolutionary movements in other countries to indicate that the Chinese Revolution has followed the pattern of other violent revolutions in creating hostility on the part of other nations. In addition there have been conflicts between Russian and Chinese wings of the Communist party throughout the world and even armed border clashes in 1969 between Soviet and Chinese troops over a piece of disputed territory.

Algeria also aroused hostility in other nations with talk of spreading the revolution to Tunisia and Morocco. It is the tendency of revolutionary movements to believe that their experience and program are so valuable that they must teach or in some cases command other countries to follow their example. The Algerians, partly because they felt they had won their independence by violence and partly because of the attention paid to them by Egypt, Cuba, China, Russia, and other countries, believed they should recommend armed revolution even in newly liberated former colonial countries which were still in the process of social change and working out their unique problems.

The Algerians tried to intervene in Angola. At first they backed the Angolan National Liberation Front (FLNA) led by Holden Roberto, but Ben Bella subsequently decided to support a rival group, the Peoples Movement for Angolan Liberation, with the result that the Angolan movements became further divided. The Portuguese benefitted by the division and the reduced pressure for independence, just as the rivalry between Chinese and Russian controlled parties creates division in some Asian and Latin American nations.

Humbaraci wrote that Egypt and Algeria had caused more "dissent between the Arab and the Black African worlds than even the most reactionary colonist diehard could have dared to hope for. This was due to their insistence that at every level, it was the Arabs who were to be the leaders of the new Africa . . ."[24]

It is not the violent aspects of revolution alone that create hostility in other nations, because communism itself is regarded as a threat to American and other business interests. Yet the violent seizure of power plus the assistance and encouragement given to other parties to do likewise in other nations does contribute to reactive hostility.

DAMAGE TO THE ECONOMY

A long period of armed violence such as occurred in both the Russian and Chinese civil wars left the economy in both countries in a seriously weakened condition. Edgar Snow reported an interview with Tsui Chung-yuan, vice-minister of education, who said of the period 1949–52: "It took us three years to rebuild the economic basis of education. Everything from transport to school was broken down. The nation was bankrupt. Money was useless; we were reduced to a barter system."[25]

During those immediate post-civil-war years it was essential to increase food production. Therefore, after the Chinese Communist party got control of China one of its first projects was agrarian reform. This meant confiscating the landlord's animals, surplus grain and tools and the distribution of his land to poor peasants. People's tribunals were set up with the power to confiscate property, arrest, imprison, and even impose sentences of execution. Similarly harsh laws were adopted against any counterrevolutionary activities. Robert North indicates that "even the most conservative estimates" of those executed as a result of these laws number several million. He wrote:

As in the Soviet Union, the human cost of this transformation

24. Humbaraci, *Algeria*, pp. 161–63.
25. Edgar Snow, *The Other Side of the River: Red China Today* (New York: Random House, Inc., 1962), p. 225.

process has been high. Undoubtedly Chinese Communist planners have increased national production—but only through intimidation and regimentation, the reduction of individual consumption (abysmally low to begin with), and the systematic employment of forced labor. Estimates of the number of individuals sentenced to forced labor . . . vary from about 14 million upward.[26]

In the Soviet Union the combination of civil war, the Allied intervention and blockade, and the peasant opposition to the requisitioning of food

had reduced agriculture to a level far below national requirements. The whole industrial system, burdened by a cumbersome and unworkable management scheme was grinding to a halt. . . . The continual decline of industry and the disorganization of transport now led step by step to the total impoverishment of the country. Each year industrial production sank to new levels until in 1920 it totaled no more than 13.2 per cent of the 1913 volume. Transportation reflected the disappearance of manufactured goods and produce of all sorts. In 1916 daily carloadings had totaled 31,164, but in 1920 the number had dwindled to 10,738.[27]

The Communists had taken the entire surplus of farm production to finance their civil war program. As a result the peasant had no incentive to produce more food than was needed by his family and his livestock. Coal production in 1918 was thirty-three percent of the amount mined in 1913. Overall industrial levels declined with some items such as pig iron being reduced to only three percent of the 1913 output. Inflation was so great that paper money was worthless and people would work or trade only for food and other needed materials.

The Communists tried everything from regulating wages

26. Robert C. North, "Peiping on the March: The Eighth Congress of the CCP," *Problems of Communism*, January–February 1957, pp. 19, 20.

27. George Vernadsky, *A History of Russia* (New Haven: Yale University Press, 1949), p. 291.

to heavy taxation, to instituting a barter system but failed to deal with the economic problem. In the end Lenin acknowledged that there had been too much control and called for a "tactical retreat." The new economic policy adopted by the tenth party congress, which lasted from 1921 to 1928, involved a return to small, private industries, to private domestic or internal trade and an end to the confiscation of farm produce. Major industry including transportation, banking, and all foreign trade continued to be state controlled. But the Communists found it necessary to appease the peasants and some others with free enterprise in order to rescue the economy.

The Algerians also suffered economically. There were at least two million unemployed Algerians at the beginning of independence in March 1962. By 1968 nearly half the work force or about five million were unemployed. The Algerians who planned the revolution had done little if any planning for the postwar economic system especially for the replacement of about eight hundred thousand Frenchmen who had been the chief technicians and administrators of Algeria.

The war-devastated economy was in such dire shape that the United States provided emergency relief in the form of food, clothing, tents, medical clinics, and personnel amounting to about $75 million between July 1, 1962 and February 1, 1963. The June 8, 1963 *Christian Science Monitor* reporting that President de Gaulle's "decision to release about $400,000, in aid to Algeria this year has saved Premier Ahmed Ben Bella's experiment in socialism from complete collapse."

Violence on a substantial scale such as occurred in Russia, China, and Algeria is damaging to agriculture and industry. It breeds further violence through starvation, labor camps, rapid industrialization, and other measures unique to each country.

FAILURE TO DEMOCRATIZE

Each of the revolutionary nations has already made significant material gains in developing agriculture, industry, science, and medicine. In both Russia and China the standard of living has risen so that no one needs to fear starvation. Women have been emancipated. Illiteracy has been wiped out. Production for use rather than for profit has been achieved. How then can it be said that there is a continuing oppression or that it is related to an earlier violence?

The charge of oppression is based on the fact that in each of the major revolutionary nations a very small group continues to determine the destiny of millions because human as well as material resources are subject to state planning. Each of the nations continues to develop its military machine including missiles and thermonuclear weapons, and each has conscription. The ruling elite is prepared to restrict, intimidate and manipulate people with the result that certain freedoms, to organize, to propagandize, to publish, to travel are denied. There are no independent labor unions, no independent judiciary and no right to participate in decision making. In Algeria there are additional liabilities such as the subordinate role of women.

These failures to liberate are not mentioned to indict revolution or communism nor are they mentioned to make other nations seem free by comparison. They are products of the authoritarian or military-type organization that was created for the efficient violent seizure of power. It can be argued, of course, that the successful seizure of power does not thereafter justify abandoning violence or a military-type organization. The mere conquest of governmental power does not destroy the exploitation or violence that has been institutionalized and accepted by the people over a period of many years under the old order. New structures must be built to replace the old even if people resist the changes. Given the fact that those who seized power did not hesitate to use violence, why should they hesitate to employ it in the reconstruction of the society they now control?

This suggests that violence may be inherent in a revolutionary regime whose original organization was planned for an efficient use of violence in seizing power. Yet at some point authoritarian controls and centralized decision making must be abandoned or new generations will face the problem of overthrowing institutionalized violence.

The fact of violence does not necessarily guarantee the failure of a revolution. It is possible, for example, eventually to overcome the economic damage caused by civil war; it is also possible to erase the hostility of other nations by successful diplomacy. It is far more difficult, however, to move from a highly centralized organizational control of the state or to abandon the use of violence against recalcitrant people. The reason is this: the violence required for an armed seizure of power in a modern industrial state or even in a large semiindustrialized nation is usually of such a magnitude that it adversely conditions the organization that must both seize power and manage the revolution thereafter. There seems to be a carry-over not only into the political structure that the revolution builds, but also into the relationships of those who control the new organization of society.

Organizations which plan and use armed violence to accomplish decentralization and democratization of power usually discover that violence is not an instrument of precision which results in the goal sought. Neither is it conducive to teaching respect for persons on which democracy depends. The end to a considerable degree is conditioned by the means.

6

THE CUBAN REVOLUTION: A CASE STUDY

THE CUBAN REVOLUTION was the result of a long series of grievances that included an American military occupation following the Spanish-American War and U.S. military interventions in 1900, 1912, 1917, and 1920. The occupation which ended in 1902 left as a legacy land laws that deprived many Cuban peasants of land while making it possible for large U.S. corporations to accumulate vast acreages.

In 1933 when the army withdrew its support from General Gerardo Machado and University of Havana students led the opposition to his despotic rule, Dr. Ramón Grau San Martín became president. His government moved to establish an agrarian reform program, a minimum wage for cutting sugar cane, a reduction in electricity rates and other reforms. There were quarrels among those who ousted Machado and a refusal by President Franklin D. Roosevelt to recognize the Grau regime during his four months in office. With U.S. encouragement, Sergeant Fulgencio Batista, who had earlier seized control of the army, forced the Grau government to resign in January 1934.

The new administration of President Mendieta was recognized within five days after he took office. Batista won election as president in 1940 and after his term of office left the country temporarily. In 1952, prior to new elections, Batista, who saw he could not win by votes, seized control of the government. Then Fidel Castro, a young lawyer, filed a brief in Cuba's courts asking that the Batista regime be declared illegal. When this challenge failed, Castro and others on July 26, 1953, attacked the Moncada barracks in Santiago. He was defeated, imprisoned, and subsequently amnestied in 1955. He went from exile in Mexico to Cuba to prepare for a second attack on the Batista regime.

Castro with eighty-one others sailed from Mexico on an old yacht, *Granma*, in November 1956. Of those who set sail only about twelve reached the Sierra Maestra in Cuba. In March 1957 a Santiago underground leader provided Castro with fifty-eight additional armed men. From 1957 until January 1, 1959, when the July 26 movement took over Cuba, the small groups of Castro's followers cultivated the peasants, engaged in sabotage and in quick hit-and-run attacks on towns with army depots, and also fought Batista's men who had been sent into the mountains. During much of the time Castro's men numbered only about three hundred.[1] They numbered only about nine hundred to a thousand at the time of their victory.

Castro won not so much by small successful battles as by the failure of Batista to gain or maintain support from the middle class and the army. When Batista was unable to stop the Castro revolt and destroy his small forces, he began a system of terror that included torture, murder, and brutality of various sorts. Batista knew that Castro and other leaders of the revolt were led by intellectuals or students, not peasants or workers. There had also been a

1. C. Wright Mills, *Listen Yankee: The Revolution in Cuba* (New York: Ballantine Books, Inc., 1960), p. 49.

student movement in the 1930s known as *Directorio Revolucionario* which was revived in 1955 by José Antonio Echeverria. That group on March 13, 1957, attacked the president's palace hoping to kill Batista. Instead they were shot in the process. From this point on, Batista's regime engaged in open repression. Moderate critics of Batista and especially students became the victims of the secret police and the army. There was a school strike which started in Santiago as a protest against the murder of two sixteen-year-old boys. "Wholesale arrests of teachers began; twenty-five teachers were seized at a single military school near Havana accused of spreading subversion among their pupils."[2] There were urban resistance attacks in Havana, Santiago, and other cities during June and July 1957, and early in 1958. Havana was without electricity and water for three days and the international airport was gutted. These attacks were not led by Castro or his organization but by middle-class civilians.

In 1958 Batista postponed the June elections until November and asked his congress for a state of "national emergency so that he might take whatever measures seemed necessary."[3] The revulsion against the Batista terror together with the corruption and the illegality of the Batista regime had destroyed even the apathy of many middle-class Cubans. The civilian disaffection had a very important influence on the army so that it had no heart for the various offensives against the small band of revolutionaries. "The real victor in this struggle was not Castro's [little army] but the entire Cuban people. The heaviest losses were suffered by the largely middle class urban resistance movement, which secreted the political and psychological acids that ate into Batista's fighting force."[4] Approximately

2. Robert Taber, *M–26 Biography of a Revolution* (New York: Lyle Stuart, 1961), p. 226.

3. Ibid., p. 227.

4. Theodore Draper, *Castro's Revolution: Myths and Realities* (New York: Praeger, 1962), p. 14.

twenty thousand civilians were killed by Batista's terror whereas far fewer of Castro's men and peasants friendly to him were killed by Batista's army.[5]

The revolution was won when Batista's generals persuaded him to leave Cuba because the army was not prepared to fight the Cuban people. Major General Cantilla was left in command of the armed forces and Carlos Manuel Piedro, senior justice of the Supreme Court, was named Batista's successor. When the news of Batista's flight reached Castro he asked his troops to head for Santiago. That city surrendered without armed violence. Camilo Cienfuegos, one of Castro's chief officers, went to Camp Columbia, the armed forces headquarters, and took command of the armed forces. Fidel Castro appointed Dr. Manuel Urrutia, a former judge, as provisional president, and began a triumphal march across Cuba to Havana. In the meanwhile the *Directorio Revolucionario* preceded the Castro troops and took over the presidential palace in Havana.[6] When Che Guevara entered the city at the head of about six hundred men there was an immediate problem of what to do with the *Directorio*. Castro, after a speech for unity delivered on January 8 in Camp Columbia, succeeded in bringing the *Directorio* into the July 26 movement. Thereafter Castro was in full control, although there were a few weeks of political confusion.

The first government appointed by Castro was composed of middle-class intellectuals. Castro preferred to be the power behind the government. His regime began, as Batista's had ended, with executions. "Swift justice overtook fifty such men in Santiago in a single day; bulldozers covered over their mass grave." The island was combed for those who had tortured and killed anti-Batista Cubans.[7]

Accounts about the executions and trials vary. Leftist

5. Leo Huberman and Paul M. Sweezy, *Cuba: Anatomy of a Revolution* (New York: Monthly Review, 1960), p. 73.
6. Taber, *Biography of a Revolution*, pp. 292–95.
7. Ibid., p. 308.

reports indicate that about seven hundred persons were shot and some twenty-five hundred persons were imprisoned. They indicate that there were trials, swift to be sure, but no mob vengeance.[8] Those right of center emphasize that trials were simply formalities because a policy of executions had been decided in advance. One case that has sometimes been cited was a trial of forty-three pilots and others who had been in Batista's air force. They had been charged with bombing villages and cities in Oriente province during the revolt. Fidel Castro had instructed the prosecution to demand a verdict of death. The court, however, felt there was insufficient evidence to convict and therefore acquitted the fliers. "In Havana, Fidel Castro heard the news and flew into a rage. He ordered the verdict set aside" and removed from the court Major Felix Peña, a commander of the rebel army who had been the presiding officer of the court. Castro "again demanded the death penalty." In the second trial the court sent the men to prison for terms of twenty to thirty years. Not long afterwards Felix Peña was found "at Camp Columbia with a bullet through his heart." The defense counsel for the fliers, Dr. Carlos Peña Justiz, was later "imprisoned as a counter-revolutionary."[9]

The Castro revolution was violent, but there was greater violence on Batista's part. One left-of-center estimate placed the number of deserters captured, wounded, and killed "at about ten percent of Batista's army" during the offensive against the rebels in Oriente.[10] Batista's army numbered over thirty thousand.

The Cuban Revolution is more difficult to analyze than some others because it is more recent, events are still continuing to unfold, and because so much that has been

8. Huberman and Sweezy, *Cuba*, pp. 71–73.

9. James Monahan and Kenneth O. Gilmore, *The Great Deception: The Inside Story of How the Kremlin Took over Cuba* (New York: Farrar, Straus, and Company, 1963), pp. 30, 31.

10. Huberman and Sweezy, *Cuba*, p. 68.

written about it is so highly partisan. Nevertheless enough is known about Cuba during the decade after the revolution to indicate that it has followed the same general pattern as other violent revolutions.

The Power Struggle. After the initial executions following Batista's flight the Castro regime gave every appearance of being a middle class or bourgeois one, with political, social, and economic freedom in which Castro was prepared to grant rights to the professional and owning classes so long as the lot of the peasants was also improved.

One of the early evidences of Castro's elimination of anyone who might oppose his ideas or rule occurred in July 1959, when Castro by a scathing public denunciation of President Urrutia stirred the people to demand his resignation. Castro did this publicly in spite of the fact that Urrutia had tried several times in the preceding months to resign his post. Since Castro's attack was on television and was seen and heard by the president, Urrutia sent his resignation to Castro while he was still speaking. Instead of accepting it Castro ordered it returned and submitted to the cabinet. Privately Castro said, "Everything must be done to keep this from looking like an overthrow."[11] Castro chose in Urrutia's place, Osvaldo Dorticós Torrado, who was much more to the left.[12]

The second major figure eliminated by Castro was Hubert Matos who had risen to the highest rank (major) in the revolution and who was put in charge of the military in Camagüey province after the victory. He objected to Communists being placed in key posts in the provincial and local governments instead of the July 26 movement people. When such replacements occurred in the rebel army he resigned his post on October 19, 1959, after trying in vain

11. Rufo Lopez-Fresquet, *My Fourteen Months With Castro* (New York: World Publishing Company, 1966), pp. 125, 126.
12. K. S. Karol, *Guerrillas in Power, The Course of the Cuban Revolution* (New York: Hill & Wang, 1970), pp. 182–83.

to discuss the problem with Castro. A majority of the army leaders in his province and others in the July 26 movement resigned also. Matos was arrested the next day. Another colleague of Castro's, one of the original twelve survivors of the invasion of Cuba, Camilo Cienfuegos, who had been made head of the Cuban Army, was sent to talk to Matos after he had offered his resignation. Immediately after the arrest of Matos, Cienfuegos disappeared. His disappearance was officially attributed to a plane accident but some thought he was becoming too popular with the people and that his disappearance was no accident.[13]

Matos was charged with treason, with having led a revolt against the government. Castro himself served as prosecutor with the inevitable result that Matos was convicted and sentenced to twenty years in prison. The political situation in Cuba at the time would not have permitted execution of one of the early revolutionaries. A group within Castro's cabinet who also had misgivings about increasing Communist influence felt the action taken against Matos was unjust. One of the cabinet, the former head of the Havana underground, Faustino Perez, refused to sign a cabinet statement labeling Matos a traitor. A private meeting of six members of the cabinet where the danger of communism was discussed was reported to Castro. Castro met with the cabinet and told them "that no revolutionary had the right to resign" whereupon Faustino Perez said that *he* had already resigned. Castro refused to accept it and instead threw Perez out of the cabinet. Then Manuel Ray, the minister of transportation, said "that he doubted the truth of the accusation that had been brought against Matos." At this point "Castro, completely out of control, told him that he, too, was out of the government."[14]

Matos's crime was simply that his resignation might

13. Lopez-Fresquet, *My Fourteen Months*, pp. 57–59; Irving Peter Pflaum, *Tragic Island* (Englewood Cliffs, N.J.: Prentice-Hall, Inc., 1961), p. 60.
14. Lopez-Fresquet, *My Fourteen Months*, pp. 150, 151.

have set an example which would have spread throughout Cuba. Matos's sentence of twenty years, which has not been commuted, can be contrasted with the fifteen-year sentence of Fidel Castro for leading an attack on the Moncado barracks. The Batista regime subsequently released Castro.

Another major revolutionary figure ousted by Castro was David Salvador who coordinated those labor groups resisting Batista and was the key representative of the underground group, Labor Unity. He was in jail during the last part of Batista's dictatorship. The Communists on the other hand went along with Batista until February 1958, when they first made contact with the Castro movement, but did not support the National Labor Front, a Castro movement led· by Salvador. In April 1958, when the urban labor groups had been asked to have a general strike, the Communists wanted a central strike committee to lead it, but the Castro labor underground refused to collaborate with the Communists. The strike was a failure, partly because the Communists did not join in it. A meeting was held on May 2, 1958, in the Sierra where Che Guevara attacked Faustino Perez and David Salvador for their noncollaboration with the Communists.[15]

Nevertheless after Batista fled, David Salvador became secretary general of the Cuban Confederation of Labor (CTC) and the leader of the Cuban labor movement for the Castro forces. At the CTC national congress which the July 26 movement dominated, Castro appeared and demanded the inclusion of the Communist candidate, Jesús Soto, in the CTC leadership. About a year later when David Salvador tried to leave Cuba he was thrown into prison without a trial.[16]

Step by step Castro eliminated rivals or those who might become obstacles to his complete dictatorship. Of the twenty persons who formed the revolutionary government eight are in exile, eight others live in Cuba but have been

15. Karol, *Guerrillas in Power*, pp. 151–53.
16. Draper, *Castro's Revolution*, pp. 25, 26, 143.

deposed, one was executed, one died in an accident, one attempted suicide and has disappeared, and the other, Dorticós, was made president.[17]

When the question is raised as to why no elections have been held as Castro promised prior to his victory, the answer generally is that Castro is so popular he would be elected anyhow. Certainly at the outset the reason for no elections was not fear that Castro would be defeated but that "the institutionalization of the democratic system would have hindered his future plans."[18] It would have been much more difficult under a democratic system to dispose of opponents, for example.

Castro not only eliminated his opponents but he also destroyed institutions that in any way could hinder him. He destroyed the labor unions "to remove all danger of strikes for higher wages and to make a wage freeze possible. . . ."[19]

In spite of his formal guarantee in the July 1957 manifesto to preserve freedom of the press and all civil liberties provided in the 1940 constitution, Castro also destroyed any semblance of a free press. He began with charges against Luis Conte Agüero, his classmate and biographer who was a prorevolutionary radio and TV commentator. Conte Agüero in one of his broadcasts appealed to Castro to keep the Communists from taking over the revolution. He was barred by militia from making his next TV appearance. When he heard Castro attack him and destroy his reputation in a four-hour TV speech, he sought asylum in the Argentine embassy and later left Cuba. Thereafter other newspapers, radio and TV stations were closed or controlled by the government.[20]

The Castro destruction of all who stood in his way eventually was extended to the Communist leaders with whom

17. Lopez-Fresquet, *My Fourteen Months*, pp. 77, 78.
18. Ibid., p. 23.
19. Pflaum, *Tragic Island*, p. 157.
20. Ibid., pp. 60–67; Monahan and Gilmore, *The Great Deception*, pp. 91–96.

he had allied his movement. Castro and his inner circle who wanted to make a model socialist state in Cuba that would be attractive to Latin Americans, at first "deferred to their comrades in the PSP (Communist Party), those experts in Marxism who knew better than anyone how to mobilize the workers and track down counterrevolutionaries."[21] But in 1962 with severe shortages in agriculture and industry and rising discontent, Castro decided he had made a mistake, denounced Aníbal Escalante, one of the chief leaders, and sent him to Russia. Again in 1968 Castro expelled Aníbal Escalante and ten other leaders of the old PSP from the Communist party. The PSP was abandoned following a process that led Castro and his colleagues to join the Integrated Revolutionary Organizations (ORI) formed in 1961, which included PSP, and to form the United Party of the Socialist Revolution (PURS) in 1963. PURS in turn was the transition to the Communist partly of Cuba in 1965 which Castro dominates.

Aníbal Escalante was also sentenced to fifteen years in prison and eight of the others to lesser terms. It was obvious from the trials that Castro again wanted to eliminate opposition, because the crimes of which they were accused included disagreement with Castro's foreign and domestic policies and establishment of a faction within the Communist party. Since these were not crimes in any legal sense it would have been reasonable in a dictatorship to expel them from the party. But to put them in prison for their ideology reveals how far Castro was prepared to go to penalize opposition.[22]

Still others, including old comrades of Castro in the Moncada barracks assault, have been imprisoned for years merely for saying something derogatory about Castro. Gustavos Arios, a former Ambassador to Belgium who had been with Castro at Moncada, was sentenced to fifteen years allegedly for saying that Castro is "crazy in the head

21. Karol, *Guerrillas in Power*, p. 540.
22. Ibid., pp. 469, 470.

and for having sent some of the money he earned to friends and relations overseas."[23]

There is no question that the Cuban Revolution follows the pattern of a strong leader who eliminates opposition either on his way to dictatorship or when his dictatorship is challenged even in an embryonic way.

The Economy. In the early years following the revolution, visitors who uncritically accepted what enthusiastic *fidelistas* said about the accomplishments of the new regime reported an improved economy. They did this on the basis of such improvements as price-control laws which reduced rents up to fifty percent, electricity and telephone rates, and the cost of medicine. They also described housing projects, beaches, shopping centers, playgrounds, and auditoriums. Some ten thousand housing units were started during 1959. There is no intent to minimize these or other accomplishments in indicating that the revolution also damaged the economy. For example, in 1958, a wartime year, Cuban exports were $733,519,000 compared to an average of $589,096,200 for the immediate postrevolutionary years of 1959 through 1963. In 1964 the exports rose to $713,825,000 but by 1966 were down again to $593,-000,000. Imports for all years through 1966 were steadily over $700 million but this meant a growing trade deficit. There are even more serious implications than a trade deficit. When Cuba nationalized American-owned industry and land, the United States imposed an embargo on Cuba. This meant that Cuban exports to the U.S. and other non-Communist countries, which accounted for 97.8 percent of Cuba's total volume in 1959, had fallen to 18.0 percent by 1962. The various Communist countries in 1962 were taking 82.0 percent of Cuba's exports.[24]

These figures, even though the Cuban ratio of trade with non-Communist countries has improved since 1962, indi-

23. Ibid., p. 474.
24. Karol, *Guerrillas in Power*, pp. 586, 587.

cate that Cuba has not been liberated from great power economic domination. It has simply exchanged one imperialism for another. The dependence of Cuba on the Soviet Union can be seen in the fact that Soviet aid to Cuba is more than a million dollars a day.[25]

The revolution which wanted to be rid of relations with the U.S. thus led to a machine crisis when new machinery and spare parts had to be ordered from the Soviet Union or its allies. Che Guevara said in August 1961 "that the reserves of raw materials were so low that the slightest trouble on the high seas brought on some kind of crisis and 'any delay of a couple of boats provokes the paralyzation of many industries.' "[26]

Another serious result of the revolution was the driving of Cuba into a monoculture of sugar. The pre-Castro economy was moving away from dependence on sugar to more cultivation of rice, coffee, beans, other vegetables, and fruits, as well as tobacco and cattle. Castro continued the process until about 1963. Then a combination of a very high world price for sugar and the need for dollars led Castro to concentrate on sugar at the expense of other crops. The export of sugar earned foreign currency, whereas the cultivation of fruits and vegetables merely helped Cubans, and any excess would have had to be transported to Eastern Europe. Since so much of Cuba's sugar crop and other exports are tied up in barter arrangements with the Soviet bloc, it became necessary to expand sugar production to get the equivalent of dollars from the non-Communist world. One reason this became necessary is the mechanization of agriculture including sugar cane. Much of the mechanized equipment had to come from Western Europe either because prices were cheaper or the equipment better. For example, Cuba ordered a thousand Soviet cane-cutting machines in 1963 only to discover that

25. Ibid., p. 425.
26. Draper, *Castro's Revolution*, p. 128.

they could not be used on Cuban terrain without destroying the crops.[27]

The concentration on sugar thus increased the Cuban trade deficit, made necessary the depriving of other sectors of the economy of investment, and also required the transfer of students from school and urban workers from their jobs in order to cut sugar cane during the much longer harvest period.

On March 12, 1962, as shortages increased, rationing was put into effect for most foods and clothing. On June 22, a law was proclaimed listing penalties for hoarding food. These laws reflected the reduced yield of rice, sorghum, sugar, and other crops, especially those in the state-owned farms. A French agronomist, Professor René Dumont, who was a Castro sympathizer, went to Cuba on a number of occasions. He wrote: "After progressing in 1959–60 due above all to a better distribution, the level of Cuban life stagnated in 1961; and it fell perhaps 15 to 20 percent in 1962 with strict rationing." The problem, he wrote, was due to the centralized direction of the economy.[28]

Another observer, James Nelson Goodsell, Latin American correspondent for the *Christian Science Monitor*, wrote in the November 1970 *Progressive* about the serious economic crisis. Castro's July 26, 1970, speech, he said, outlined the following problems: "a serious labor shortage, low worker productivity, growing absenteeism in some factories, an unfavorable balance of trade, lack of new machinery and inefficient transportation services." Castro said specifically that he believed that "the revolution is faced by a challenge greater than any it has faced before."

Apparently the discontent which has existed in the cities for some time has also begun to grow in the country. Goodsell wrote:

27. Karol, *Guerrillas in Power*, pp. 412, 417, 421–23.
28. René Dumont, *Cuba: Socialisme et Developpement* (Paris: Editions du Seuil, 1964), p. 91.

A Cuban peasant who told me he had been "for Fidel for a long time" and felt that "Fidel genuinely tried at first to make things better for us" added that he is not so sure today: "Our life hasn't changed much, despite the promises and the early improvements. Life is still hard, whether Batista rules or Fidel rules."

The Cuban economy has suffered as a direct result of the revolution, which included too rapid nationalization, elimination of much of the tourist industry, the U.S. embargo, centralized direction of the economy, dependence on the Soviet Union, discontent due to alienating urban workers and the middle class by adopting communism and totalitarian methods. Since Cuba had one of the highest standards of living in Latin America, even better than that of Japan, the problem Castro faced was improving the standard sufficiently so as to justify the revolution.

Centralization of Power. Power being centralized in the army and bureaucracy, which we have noted following other violent revolutions, has also occurred in Cuba. Just after the revolution Cubans were organized in workers' militia. Then Fidel Castro felt so secure that he boasted of distributing guns to everyone. The militia has subsequently been changed into a Civil Defense Organization directly controlled by the army. No longer is there a "people's army." Even the guns are taken to the barracks and locked up after each military drill or training exercise.[29] The people were also militarized when the country was reorganized on the model of its army. "Command posts" led by members of the Political Bureau were set up in every province to coordinate the great agricultural "battle." Labor brigades were turned into battalions, each divided into three squads, led by a major and a chief of operations responsible for discipline and work progress. Motorized battalions were formed.[30] In 1967 a special "invasion bri-

29. Karol, *Guerrillas in Power*, p. 457.
30. Ibid., p. 445.

gade" was formed and named after Che Guevara. "The brigade was under direct army control."[31]

Castro, in order to deal with his domestic problems, has introduced military conscription as well as labor conscription.[32] All workers have to carry labor cards. These were introduced in September 1969 to cut absenteeism and so that all infractions of discipline could be noted on each card.[33]

A centralized bureaucracy has also developed. There is a planning board, a ministry of industries, and a department of agricultural production, all of which are involved in centralized direction of the economy. A bureaucracy of this sort is inevitable in a dictatorship that tries to manage almost everything. Since Castro came to power there have been no elections. Everyone both in all the offices of the Communist party and in all the state offices is appointed by Fidel Castro or others close to him. This does not mean that Castro and Guevara were unaware of the dangers of bureaucracy. Guevara writing in *Cuba Socialista* for February 1963 said, ". . . after the triumph of the revolution, the evil of bureaucracy begins to proliferate greatly." In 1967 Castro called upon the people to fight against bureaucracy.

International Hostility. The Cuban Revolution followed the pattern of other violent upheavals in posing a threat to other countries. The first activity against Cuba came as a result of the refugees who fled Cuba before and after Batista's flight. By 1961 more than a hundred thousand Cuban refugees had entered the United States.[34] Since 1964 an airlift operated by Americans with Castro's consent has brought 150 Cubans a week to Florida. There are an estimated seven hundred thousand who still want to

---

31. Ibid.
32. Ibid., p. 535.
33. Ibid., p. 517.
34. Draper, *Castro's Revolution*, p. 61.

leave, according to Leo Huberman and Paul Sweezy in *Socialism in Cuba* (1969).

These refugees plus the Cuban move toward communism and subsequently the expropriation of North American-owned enterprises led to the Bay of Pigs invasion on April 17, 1961. That invasion led in turn to the Russian missiles being brought to Cuba and the missile crisis of October 21–28, 1962, when the United States demanded the dismantling of the missiles and prepared for war if they remained. The withdrawal of the missiles by a unilateral decision of the Russians resulted in a serious division between the Communist parties in the rest of Latin America and the partisans of Castro, with the Communists emphasizing peaceful coexistence instead of revolution. The withdrawal of the Russian missiles plus the continued American embargo made it clear to Castro that Cuba could survive only in the Soviet Union's camp.

The Cuban move into the Communist camp plus strong North American pressure made it possible for the U.S. to secure the expulsion of Cuba from the Organization of American States by a vote of fourteen to six in January 1962. Cuba had already tried to stir up revolution in Latin America by enlarging Cuban embassies and consulates and establishing relations with all centers of opposition to those governments. Cuban friendship societies were formed in those countries and persons were recruited for training in Cuba. As a result of such actions, diplomatic relations with Cuba were broken by Costa Rica and Panama in 1961. In November 1960, a group of anti-Communists led by a Cuban refugee raided the Cuban embassy in Peru at the end of a working day. The confidential documents seized and copied were made available to the Peruvian government, which broke diplomatic relations on December 31, 1960.

Documents stolen from the Cuban embassy in Buenos Aires contained instructions for training guerrillas, for espionage and sabotage, as well as stirring up unrest in unions and among students. The result was a rupture of diplomatic relations with Cuba in February 1962.[35]

The attempts at Cuban promotion of disaffection in Latin America plus the revolution itself led the United States to place a greater emphasis on influencing Latin American armed forces. Latin armies have become more political, thus leading to increasing military control over political life. The U.S. brought many Latin American officers not only to various armed forces schools in the U.S., such as the Army War College at Leavenworth, Kansas, but also to schools in the Canal Zone specializing in counterinsurgency training.

The example of the Cuban revolution thus encouraged the formation of guerrilla movements in Latin America and led the United States to a large-scale program designed to prevent any future Cuban-type revolutions. Unquestionably the Cuban example had something of a causal influence on events in the Dominican Republic, including the American intervention of April and May 1965.[36]

Continuing Oppression. The revolution in Cuba did not result in liberation from oppression. Instead, one ruling group gave way to another. Batista was replaced by Castro. The North American imperialists and their Cuban friends were replaced by the Cuban Communist party and the Russian imperialists. This shift in power was manifest in many ways. Under Batista in 1939 the Communists in return for their support were permitted to form an officially recognized Cuban Confederation of Labor (CTC) with Lázaro Peña as its secretary general. Castro followed Batista's example in 1961 by putting Lázaro Peña in office as secretary general of the CTC for essentially the same purpose, to have a docile labor movement. Instead of pro-

35. Monahan and Gilmore, *The Great Deception*, pp. 164–70.

36. Julio Cesar Martínez, "Revolution and Counter Revolution in the Dominican Republic: The Chessboard," *New Politics* 4, no. 2 (Spring 1965), pp. 47, 48.

viding for free trade unions, Castro and other middle-class intellectuals in 1963 divided the working class into sub-groups and graded them for purposes of wages that could be earned only if certain norms were fulfilled. The wage scale resulted in a reduction of hourly income from an average of ninety cents to seventy-five cents.[37]

The government has established wide income differentials partly to keep technicians from leaving. One pro-Castro observer complained at the luxury restaurants where a meal costs a couple between twenty and forty dollars and long lines wait outside these places to be served. "Paradoxically all this luxury has increased by leaps and bounds since Cuba launched its campaign for greater equality and the training of the *hombre neuvo*."[38]

The introduction of compulsory military service came after the missile crisis and after President Kennedy had given Khrushchev assurances of no direct invasion by the U.S. It was introduced after Castro had claimed that he could now announce a "situation of security." When Castro's brother Raúl presented the conscription law, he said that since recruits would receive only seven pesos a month, the government would profit from the substantial savings in soldiers' salaries. Youths between seventeen and twenty years of age were drafted for a three-year term and put to work picking coffee beans and cutting sugar cane. Raúl Castro justified the three-year term on the basis of labor utility. The Cuban Army was not only divided into workers and soldiers, but the government had a new source of cheap labor.[39]

The Castro government has also established labor camps on the Soviet model except that persons are sent there as a kind of administrative punishment for transgressions that are not punishable as crimes. The May 1963 report of the

37. Theodore Draper, *Castroism: Theory and Practice* (New York: Praeger, 1965), pp. 183, 187.
38. Karol, *Guerrillas in Power*, pp. 430, 431.
39. Draper, *Castroism*, pp. 174, 175.

Inter-American Commission on Human Rights of the Organization of American States revealed that the Cuban concentration camp system "shows many of the features that characterized and still characterize the concentration camps in some totalitarian countries—such as barbed-wire fences, rudimentary barracks for shelter, and the infliction of corporal punishment and constant forced labor."[40]

Under Castro, Cuban justice has become worse than under Batista. Revolutionary tribunals have been set up composed of politically trustworthy persons. In March 1963 Law No. 1098 was proclaimed which provides for imprisonment of twenty to thirty years for stealing as little as $100. Stories have appeared in the press such as one in *Hoy* November 19, 1963, of Mario Sosa Hernández being sentenced to twenty years in prison for stealing about a hundred pesos worth of fruits and vegetables.[41]

Those who are pleased with the results of the Cuban Revolution generally point to the very important programs begun by Castro in the early part of his regime such as the new medical clinics, new schools, and elimination of graft in government. It is interesting to note that the U.S. State Department which is usually not unduly concerned with the liberation of people in dictatorial regimes allied with the U.S., nevertheless correctly appraised these social programs in a white paper on Cuba. That paper said: "the record of the Castro regime has been a record of the steady and consistent betrayal of Dr. Castro's pre-revolutionary promises; and the result has been to corrupt the social achievements and make them the means, not of liberation, but of bondage."

As for human rights there is no right to vote, to organize political parties, to establish free labor unions, to maintain a free press, to petition representatives in government, or to be tried by an independent judiciary. Theodore Draper indicates that copies of Boris Pasternak's *Doctor Zhivago*

40. Ibid., pp. 178–80.
41. Ibid., pp. 181–82.

had been banned by the government and confiscated from a Havana bookshop as counterrevolutionary literature.[42] Campaigns have been undertaken against poets and dramatists such as Heberto Padilla and Antony Arrufat. The government published their prize-winning works with a critical preface and dismissed Padilla from his job.[43]

If one assumes that man lives by bread or material achievements alone it could be argued that the Cuban peasants are eating as well or better than under Batista. But if the goal of the revolution was the ending of oppression, there is little evidence of achievement.

New Form of Dependency. The Cuban Revolution as we have noted has not humanized or democratized the revolutionaries or their heirs. Necessity to break even, let alone improve the economy, has resulted in acceptance of the Soviet model at many points in Cuba. There was even an imitation of Mao's Cultural Revolution when Castro unleashed the people to take direct action on various private shops, kiosks, and self-employed craftsmen. His Great Revolutionary Offensive resulted in the confiscation of consumer goods, the closing of 16,634 private enterprises in Havana, and the forcing of 9,179 craftsmen to work in factories.[44] In addition to the labor camps, labor conscription, the brutal penal system, and the death penalty for burning sugar cane, Castro has demonstrated his acceptance of dehumanization without protest in the following incidents: He did not protest the use by the Mexican government of tanks and troops in 1968 to break up a peaceful demonstration of students which left more than three hundred killed and two thousand wounded. Cuban athletes participated in the Olympic Games in Mexico shortly thereafter. Castro did not protest the invasion of Czechoslovakia in August 1968 by Soviet troops but endorsed it as necessary.

42. Ibid., p. 86.
43. Karol, *Guerrillas in Power*, p. 449.
44. Ibid., pp. 441, 442.

Counterrevolutionary Tendencies. As a general rule violent revolutions also generate violent counterrevolutions. It could be asserted that the Bay of Pigs invasion and some other abortive attempts to unseat Castro were the only counterrevolutionary efforts made. But a case can be made also to the effect that the increasing authoritarian rule by Fidel Castro and his acceptance of the Soviet domestic model and Soviet foreign policy are so contrary to the goals of the Cuban Revolution as to be counterrevolutionary. Some might defend Castro's increasing repression as economically necessary because of the actions and attitudes of the United States. But guilty as North American governments have been and are for imperialism and other systems of violence, it is still not possible to absolve Castro's repression as simply a reaction to the United States. Castro's takeover in Cuba was largely unhindered by the United States. The U.S. cannot be blamed for Castro's treatment of Matos or his colleagues in the first revolutionary government or for his first flirtation and collaboration with the Communist party or for all of the Cuban exiles who originally backed the revolution. Neither can the U.S. be blamed for a sudden wholesale expropriation of foreign property instead of one calculated to avoid equally hasty action in reprisal. Castro was understandably angry, but it was unnecessary to turn against old colleagues or to accept the reactionary ideology and methods of the Soviet Union. It is still too early to make a clear judgment about the Cuban Revolution. The Cuban people have accepted repression before. If they become convinced that Castro's regime has moved away from its revolutionary purpose, only events will indicate whether they will passively accept it or try an overthrow.

Romanticism. The Cuban Revolution has been justified and romanticized not only in Cuba but in many other countries. In Cuba there is the same kind of romantic adoration of Fidel Castro that there was of Stalin during his lifetime. From the very beginning Castro cultivated the people by traveling around the country and listening to their needs. Jean Paul Sartre, Paul Baron, and other visitors to Cuba coined or first used the phrase "direct democracy" to describe the dialogue between Castro and the ordinary people which kept him informed of problems if he had the inclination to solve them. This phrase "direct democracy" in itself is a romanticism of paternalism, to use a mild term, or for dictatorship. Yet many Cubans who grumble at conditions assume that if Castro only knew he would change things.

Numerous foreign visitors to Cuba record their praises of the achievements of the revolution. Few report the tremendous problems facing Cuba or the injustice done to the people or analyze the meaning of a revolution so largely dependent on one man. It was the entire Cuban people who suffered at the hands of the Batista regime and North American imperialism, yet the people are not now participants in decision making. It is the charismatic leader who decides and the people who implement or drag their feet.

Undoubtedly there are good and bad aspects of the Cuban Revolution. Until this writer talked with leftist Cuban refugees and began serious investigation of the critical as well as favorable aspects there was an assumption that the Castro Revolution was different: minimal violence, great leader, positive programs, and on balance a more humanizing result. So great was the romanticism about Castro in liberal and left-wing circles in Latin America and in the U.S., that it was a surprise to discover left-of-center writers such as K. S. Karol who were seriously questioning in 1969 and 1970 the course of the revolution after initial, almost wholly favorable, appraisals.

Certainly the Cuban Revolution is so recent that a long historical look is impossible. But fourteen years and acceptance of a new imperialism provides more information as to the direction of Cuba than the early simplistic approval of an apparently successful elimination of North American imperialism.

7

LATIN AMERICAN SYMBOLS
OF REVOLUTION

THE TWO CHIEF SYMBOLS of violent revolution in Latin America are Che Guevara and Camilo Torres. Both were killed in the course of guerrilla war against South American governments. Che is more widely known and his influence more widely felt in secular circles, whereas Camilo Torres, a Roman Catholic priest, has become known throughout Latin America, especially in Catholic circles. Because of the myths which surround their names it is important to take a look at each of them and their contributions, or their failures. As history has so often noted, an untimely death, especially at the hands of an assassin or an unpopular government, is likely to make even a dead man's failures or poor judgment into a success story. Liberation ethics, however, is not based on romanticism or irrationality but on methods that are related to probable consequences.

CHE GUEVARA

No other name has stirred radical youth in both South and North America as has that of Che Guevara. At one time, before Fidel Castro became so dependent on the Soviet Union and began to follow the Soviet line, Castro might have taken first place. But the combination of Castro's subservience and Che's martyrdom made Guevara preeminent especially among those who look at revolution romantically.

Ernesto Che Guevara made his basic reputation in the guerrilla warfare in Cuba prior to Batista's flight. Since that Cuban campaign he had no major successes either during his Cuban political career or in his attempts to export the Cuban Revolution. His failures began while he was in charge of the ministry of industries. He made so many mistakes, which he acknowledged, that the Cuban economy was in serious trouble. In late 1964 he went to Africa where he vigorously attacked Soviet imperialism, thus embarrassing Castro, whose government was dependent on a Soviet subsidy of a million dollars a day. He even attacked Fidel Castro in an article which appeared in a French magazine by stating that in the battles of the Sierra Maestra campaign "Fidel Castro participated in only one and it was a complete failure."[1]

In 1965 Guevara took a group of 125 Cubans to the Congo to help the Kinshasa rebels against the government of the Democratic Republic of the Congo. The rebel group had received guerrilla training from the Algerians and weapons and supplies from the Russians. Che went to the Congo to give them the benefit of his own leadership and experience. The Cuban force, however, did not make the impact Che expected. By the fall of 1965 Che recognized his failure to make good fighters out of the Kinshasa rebels and departed for Cuba.[2]

Che Guevara's most significant failure was his Bolivian venture. It is significant in many ways. The first and

1. Daniel James, ed., *The Complete Bolivian Diaries of Ché Guevara and Other Captured Documents* (New York: Stein and Day, 1968), p. 13.
2. Ibid., p. 15.

perhaps most important meaning is that it discredits Che as a revolutionary theorist or strategist and with him Castro. The key elements in the Castro–Guevara theory of revolution include the following: (1) It is not necessary to have a revolutionary situation in Marxist terms. A capable guerrilla force can create a revolutionary situation by its very existence and dynamic activity. It serves as a *foco insurreccional* or a center for the growth of an armed revolution. (2) The best base for a guerrilla campaign is in the rural areas where peasants will support the guerrillas and before long join them. They can be persuaded to join by promises of land reform which would give them their own farms. (3) A dynamic growing guerrilla group could become strong enough to defeat a nation's army. (4) Contrary to Leninist doctrine that the Communist party directs the revolution, they believed that the guerrilla leaders and the armed revolutionary struggle should take precedence over the party. (5) The only way to achieve the necessary social change in Latin America is by armed violence.

These principles, which are set forth in Guevara's book, *Guerrilla Warfare*, and in Regis Debray's book, *Revolution in the Revolution*, as the Cuban experience or the Castro-Guevara theory, are largely romanticized versions of what happened in Cuba and not historically accurate. The small guerrilla band in Cuba did not create the revolutionary situation; it had been created earlier by popular reaction to the Batista regime, including its usurpation of power. Only a messianic complex or a failure in political analysis could have led Castro and Guevara to believe that their small band of guerrillas created the widespread disaffection in Cuba that caused the revolutionary situation. There is, however, no doubt that they provided the confrontation that crystallized and aroused the opposition to Batista. Che's failure in Bolivia was due in part to this rewriting of Cuban history and the romanticizing of the impact of Castro's band on the revolutionary situation. As a result Guevara did not think it necessary to study or analyze the political situation in Bolivia. All that was necessary in his judgment was an active band of guerrillas under his leadership and the armed revolution would spread. If Guevara had made a study of the Bolivian revolution of 1952 and the regime of President Barrientos, he would have noted great differences between the Bolivia of 1966 and the Cuba of 1956. The fact that Barrientos was a general and had come to power through a military coup may have led Che to think of him as another Batista. But Barrientos had not opposed the revolutionary trend in Bolivia as Batista had in Cuba. He had actually been a part of the revolution of 1952 and a preceding uprising led by Villarroel who laid the groundwork for agrarian reform and universal education. In 1966 Barrientos won the presidency in an apparently fair election, gaining about sixty-two percent of the vote. Nevertheless the Barrientos government was neither democratic nor revolutionary. It exiled mine union leaders and used repressive measures against the miners. Yet it was not counterrevolutionary or brutal to its political opponents and in some respects it continued policies of the previous administration which had served since the 1952 revolution.

Guevara's second assumption, that there had been a peasant base for the revolution in Cuba, was also wrong. It was the Cuban middle class who provided the major support for Castro and the major opposition to Batista. This was evident not only in the composition of Castro's first cabinet but also in the guerrilla group that fought under Castro's leadership. Some peasants did support Castro but he never had a peasant army or a peasant leader. When Guevara went to Bolivia he was able to muster about fifty persons. These were led by people of middle-class background and, aside from the Cubans, were chiefly students, unemployed miners, and taxi drivers. Even after Che organized his guerrilla groups into two striking forces there was not one *campesino* (peasant) among them. Here again Guevara had not done his homework. He evidently did not know that President Barrientos had cultivated the *campe-sinos* while he carried out his policy of restricting the tin miners. The area Che and his colleagues selected as their base was sparsely settled by *campesinos* who had owned their own land for generations and who were in no way disaffected from the government.

Instead of the peasants helping Che, they informed on him and actively opposed him. Neither the Cubans nor the Bolivians spoke the language of the region. This plus the long hair, beards, different dress, and weapons made them stand out as foreigners or at least as outsiders with nothing in common with the peasants. In short it was obvious that Che's hope of getting peasant support was not based on any study or planning but on either messianic assumption or a romantic belief that his misinterpretation or reinter-pretation of what happened in Cuba would almost auto-matically repeat itself in Bolivia.

His third assumption, based on another misreading of what happened in Cuba, was that a peasant guerrilla force could defeat the Bolivian army. Actually the Castro guer-rillas had not defeated the Cuban army. The Cuban army finally decided not to fight, because to do so would mean fighting urban middle-class Cubans as well as others with whom both soldiers and officers had ties. In Cuba also the Castro guerrillas had not yet accepted communism or pro-posed an ideology unacceptable to the middle class from which he drew his support. In Bolivia, Guevara did not have the support of miners or urban workers or the middle class and apparently did little to cultivate any of these groups. Moreover his ties with Cuban communism made him suspect even to the Bolivian Communists who fol-lowed the Russian line and looked upon the Cubans as dictating their own position.

One reason Che would have found it impossible to de-feat the Bolivian army is that so many peasants were in the army. Another is that the Bolivian army was improving its image and relationships by engaging in what the Pentagon calls "civic action" projects. These include building dams, roads, irrigation systems, or other projects visible to the peasants and rural villagers. The decisive factor that Che underestimated was the antiguerrilla training given by U.S. forces to a few hundred Bolivians who comprised the "Ranger" units that finally defeated Guevara's band. Che received no reinforcements either from Havana or Bolivia, while his opponents were receiving aid from the United States.

The fourth principle followed by Guevara, that the guerrillas lead rather than take direction from the party, alienated the Communist party leaders of Bolivia. The result was no Communist support except for a few individual party members who joined Che, and for a brief statement of solidarity.

Che's belief, which was held also by Castro and Debray, that social change would come only by armed force, is one held by many Latin Americans. They have little if any conception of nonviolent change in spite of their admiration for both Gandhi and King. However, Che apparently didn't learn from the failures of other armed revolutionaries. Argentine troops in 1964 defeated a guerrilla force led by Jorge Massetti. In Peru a peasant revolt near Cuzco led by Hugo Blanco was effectively put down, as was another guerrilla group, related to Castro, in 1965.

There are of course other reasons for holding that Che Guevara is not the romantic revolutionary hero that millions in North and South America believe he is. One of his errors stemmed from his great vanity. He was so confident that a force led by Guevara could not lose, that he and his followers not only carried cameras and darkroom equipment to develop film but took a large number of photographs so as to record their adventure for posterity. They also kept diaries. When some of these were found by the Bolivian soldiers, the authorities discovered Che's leadership, the Cuban government's sponsorship of the invasion and guerrilla activity, how the guerrillas were organized, and other details that contributed to their defeat.

Che's supreme self-confidence as well as his popularity had led to rivalry with Fidel Castro. Although Castro helped Che get started in Bolivia, he kept a strange silence about Che when he could have announced Che's need for men and supplies and political support. Che expected Castro to publicize his leadership of the guerrillas in Bolivia but Castro did not do it in spite of several opportunities such as the Latin American Solidarity Conference in July and August 1967, over which he presided. After the Bolivian army had discovered the diaries, photographs, and other material and knew of Che's role, Castro continued his silence. The only reasonable explanation is that Castro preferred not to call more attention to his only remaining rival for revolutionary leadership in Latin America.

One writer indicates that Guevara's success would have jeopardized Castro's leadership. "There can be little doubt that with a victory in Bolivia, it would have been Che, not Castro, who would have directed the projected continental revolution and emerged the greater leader."[3]

Even with Castro's help Che would probably have failed. He made many tactical mistakes such as inadequate precautions to keep his photos and documents from being discovered, or failure to damage telephone or electric lines, or to attack nearby oil fields or transportation lines. In short, his only success as a guerrilla commander was in carrying out Castro's orders during the Cuban campaign. Both in the Congo and Bolivia he showed neither strategic nor tactical ability. His Bolivian campaign as reflected in the various captured diaries reveal again and again his complete disregard of his own principles of guerrilla fighting as set forth in his book, *Guerrilla War*.

The Guevara myth of a brilliant guerrilla leader was

3. Ibid., p. 66.

preserved by his death because millions of people will re-member that he died fighting to bring revolution to the heart of South America. What is generally not understood about Che is that his guerrilla effort ending in his death seriously damaged the concept of a Cuban-type revolution to which his admirers are devoted. Che demonstrated not only to Castro but also to others that it is impossible to export or duplicate a Sierra Maestra-type revolution out-side Cuba. One of Che's French admirers wrote that Che proved "that the Cuban Revolution was an exceptional phenomenon which will never reappear in the same form, and—alas!—that revolution today can never succeed on the basis of romanticism and improvisation."[4] Castro made his own belated public acknowledgment of this truth in his speech of April 22, 1970, when he said:

When we speak of supporting a revolutionary movement, we should say that that support does not necessarily have to be expressed exclusively in favor of guerrilla movements . . . no two cases in the history of the world are exactly alike, and there will not be two revolutions that develop in the same way.[5]

Another fundamental criticism of the Guevara myth is its glorification of the revolutionary leader instead of the movement. It is thus a continuation of the Latin American tendency to admire and follow the *caudillo* (strong man) instead of insisting on rule by the people. Yet Guevara's death had in it none of the nobility or quality of other leaders in history who have been assassinated or executed. Che's arrogance was maintained to the end. When the Bolivian soldiers called for surrender a guerrilla named Willy who had been carrying Che set him on the ground and started shooting. Willy was instantly killed but Che shouted to the Bolivian troops, "Don't kill me, I'm Che

4. Jean Lartéguy, *The Guerrillas*, trans. Stanley Hockman (New York: World Publishing Company, 1970), p. 261.
5. *Problems of Communism*, July–August 1970, p. 23.

Guevara."[6] A wounded Bolivian soldier, Benito Gimenez, who was in the same shed with the captured Guevara reported that the Bolivian Ranger commander, Colonel Selnich, told Che that "he had killed a lieutenant" that Selnich "had loved like his own son." The colonel questioned Che but Guevara refused to answer. "Then Guevara slapped Selnich with his right hand [which] caught him right in the mouth." The colonel left but others continued to take care of Che's wounds until orders came from La Paz during the night to execute him. A differing account of his death reveals that he had eight bullets in his chest, was in great pain, and "was helped to his death."[7] There is little doubt, however, that Bolivian and U.S. authorities welcomed his death. Although there are people in Latin America who view Che as a new messiah or Christ who sacrificed himself, it seems clear that he did not die in the fashion of a self-effacing hero of a great cause or movement as did Jesus or Gandhi.

The Guevara failure in Bolivia made it virtually inevitable that Castro would have to accept the Soviet approach to Latin America. The collapse of the guerrilla movement downgraded Castro's prestige and judgment rather than Che's. It made obvious the fact that Castro was no longer able to export revolution to the other Latin American countries. If he was to have an influence on the continent it would have to be by example. This plus Cuba's own need made it essential for him to knuckle under to the Soviet Union. So long as he was a successful or at least a continuing political and military factor in Latin America, the Soviet Union could not have withdrawn any significant support without losing face in the entire socialist world. But Guevara, in spite of the fact that he had opposed and criticized the Soviet line, made it inevitable by his Bolivian venture that Cuba follow that line. The significance of

6. Lartéguy, *The Guerrillas*, p. 260.
7. Ibid., pp. 258–61.

Castro's change after Che's failure can be seen from his actions. In August 1967, at the Latin American Solidarity organization conference in Havana (composed chiefly of Communist revolutionaries), Castro pushed through the conference committee a resolution condemning Russian aid policies in Latin America. He also called for guerrilla warfare in Latin America contrary to Soviet policy, thus making it clear that Cuba was not a Soviet satellite and that Castro planned to determine Communist theory and action in Latin America.[8]

About ten months after Che's death, Castro began a slow retreat from the position he took at the Havana conference. By August 1968, Castro was defending the Russian invasion of Czechoslovakia preparatory to moving completely into the Soviet camp with respect to Latin American policy.

Castro's ecnomic dependence on the Soviet Union plus his endorsement of the Russian invasion of Czechoslovakia and the Soviet line in Latin America made it obvious not only that Cuba had been drawn into the orbit of another great power but that Castro would be a dependent rather than independent force in Latin America.[9]

CAMILO TORRES

A second hero of violent revolution in Latin America is Camilo Torres, a native of Colombia. He was born into the upper urban class in 1929, studied for the priesthood in the diocesan seminary of Bogotá and received an MA in social science at the University of Louvain. He returned to Colombia in 1960 and was named chaplain as well as profes-

8. *Washington Post*, 13 August 1967.
9. An excellent analysis of Che Guevara is Robert F. Lamberg, "Che in Bolivia: The 'Revolution' that Failed," *Problems of Communism,* July–August 1970, pp. 25–37. Mr. Lamberg taught for a time at the Centro de Estudios Internacionales at El Colegio de México.

sor of sociology at the University of Bogotá. He was a member of one of the twenty-four families that were most powerful in Colombia and also had the support of the Roman Catholic hierarchy. At first, after he became the leader of the students, he sought reforms and projects that might improve the lot of the people. Later he asked the hierarchy to permit academic freedom in church schools and to give up the monopoly over education exercised by the church in Colombia.

He sought free public schools financed by the state for all children. Among his other proposals were land reform, with the land cultivated through cooperative and community systems, and the nationalization of all banks, insurance companies, transportation, radio, TV, hospitals, and other health services.

After Camilo's "platform" for Colombia was made public in March 1965 the Roman Catholic cardinal, Luis Concha, archbishop of Bogotá, stated on June 18 that

the activities of Father Camilo Torres are incompatible with his sacerdotal character and with his religious habit itself. It can happen that these two circumstances induce some Catholics to follow the erroneous and pernicious doctrines which Father Torres proposes in his program.[10]

On June 24, Torres petitioned the cardinal by letter to be laicized and the cardinal on June 26 approved the request. There is evidence that the hierarchy in Colombia opposed Torres at a number of points including his position with respect to ownership of property and his advocacy of violence.

Camilo Torres in August 1965 launched a weekly newspaper with the title *Frente Unido*. His purpose was to bring unaligned groups into the United Front of revolutionary elements. But some of the groups that originally supported Torres began to withdraw when they saw that

10. German Guzman, *Camilo Torres*, trans. John D. Ring (New York, Sheed & Ward, 1969), p. 22.

his United Front included the Communist party and other Marxists. He was prepared to work with the Communists for common goals, but was not prepared to join the party.

A French writer indicated that Torres never built a movement of the nonaligned either by his newspaper or his speaking tours.

His violent tone and very *fidelistic* style provoked violence along the way . . . Camilo loved to talk before crowds. His speeches lasted three and four hours. Unfortunately he was also disorganized and one has to know how to bring these crowds together, how to transport them and put them in a proper frame of mind. . . . He had many friends but no followers. He knew nothing about political organization, the work of agitation, how to build cells and clandestine networks and prepare for a meeting. The Communists took over the organization of his tours and procured a public for him just as the public was beginning to weary of him.[11]

The Communists, however, did not want to string along indefinitely with Torres unless he accepted some discipline and gave up the idea of going with the guerrillas as he had hinted he might. They knew that Torres was romantic about the guerrillas and could do more effective work arousing and educating the masses. In the end Torres decided to abandon the Communist party of Colombia and join a smaller Castroite force of about two hundred men known as the National Liberation Army (ALN). The ALN had no real support except from Cuba or from the university, and the Communist party, which had recently gained a lot of influence with the students, was cutting off that support. The ALN or "Castroite rebellion needed a big name to relaunch" their movement and persuaded Torres to join their guerrilla band.[12]

The ALN expected Torres to establish relationships with

11. Lartéguy, *The Guerrillas*, p. 131.
12. Ibid., p. 136.

the peasants and serve as a political recruiter. But he insisted on participating in their military activity even though he had had no military or guerrilla training. Camilo Torres believed that

change implies violence for those who retain power. But violence is not excluded from the Christian ethic, because if Christianity is concerned with eliminating the serious evils which we suffer and saving us from the continuous violence in which we live without possible solution, the ethic is to be violent once and for all in order to destroy the violence which the economic minorities exercise against the people.[13]

These, his own words, reveal his naïvete about politics and revolution. To believe that one violent uprising, even if successful, would end oppression is utopianism of a Marxist-Leninist or Castro variety rather than based on Christian doctrine. Christian doctrine does not look for the Kingdom of God or any final era of no oppression as the result of one great violent revolution.

Camilo Torres sincerely believed that when he would issue the call, the nation would rise up to support him. In messianic terms he issued a call to Colombians from the mountains in January 1966 that included passages such as the following:

I want to tell the Colombian people that this is the moment; that I have not betrayed them; that I have passed through the plazas of the towns and cities campaigning for the unity and organization of the people for the seizure of power . . . I have involved myself in the armed battle. . . . All of us Colombian patriots must place ourselves at the service of the war . . . The battle of the people must become a national battle. . . .[14]

His call failed to rally Colombians to the guerrilla cause.

Although there are different versions of Camilo Torres' death on February 15, 1966, it apparently happened as a

13. Guzman, *Camilo Torres*, p. 77.
14. Ibid., pp. 240, 241.

result of a trap or ambush into which the guerrillas fell. The guerrillas saw an army patrol of seven men and attacked them. The soldiers fled and led the guerrillas into the arms of about sixty others. Torres was killed while taking a rifle from a wounded soldier.

Torres was unsuccessful while alive but immensely successful after death. During his life he failed to unite the various leftist groups around his United Front platform. These groups refused to accept him as their leader in view of his relations with the Communists. The Communists in turn were prepared to assist Torres only if they could use him. He failed to build a movement of the nonaligned. He failed to train leaders of a potential movement or to attract to his side others capable of helping him build a movement. His newspaper, *Frente Unido*, instead of uniting, polarized the various groups he wanted to unite. When he joined the ALN and issued his appeal to the nation, he did not become the rallying point for an uprising. Even on the day of his death, according to one account, he acted ingloriously. According to the soldiers who reported the battle, five of the guerrillas moved toward the fallen soldiers. When one of them started "to finish off Lieutenant González who lay on the ground" a soldier who was near shot the guerrilla, who was identified as Camilo Torres.[15]

Another account, which his biographer believes is closer to the truth, shows him as naïvely trying to pick up the rifle of a soldier after he (Torres) was wounded, contrary to the orders of the guerrilla leader who had ordered him to retreat.[16] In any event his death has been built by various revolutionary groups into a symbol or myth of Christian justification for violent révolution.

A Roman Catholic and former associate of Torres who asserts that he is now more a Marxist than a Catholic and who is engaged in recruiting and agitation for guerrilla

15. Ibid., pp. 250–51.
16. Ibid., p. 252.

forces, said in Bogotá in July 1970: "It is the duty of every Christian to participate in the Revolution or to deny his own religion. We believe that ours is the only way." Then identifying Torres as a Christ figure, he added: "A Christ in Latin America is worth more than ten generals. It is the magic incarnation of his suffering that is effective."[17] In the discussion, one of those present pointed out that there is no parallel between Torres and Jesus of Nazareth, who refused to join a violent revolutionary movement (the zealots), and who died on a cross without seeking power for any political group and without inflicting violence on anyone. Another Colombian, a Protestant clergyman who was also recruiting for the guerrillas and who had graduated from a prominent theological seminary in the United States, responded by saying that "it is wrong to imitate Christ. He is dynamic, so that he does use violence today. He is on the side of the oppressed and at war with the oppressors." A further question, "Was not Jesus concerned with the liberation of oppressors as well as the oppressed?" brought the following response: "The guerrillas are going to liberate the oppressors and the oppressed." The discussion implied that the oppressors would be liberated by death. The discussion also revealed that Camilo Torres is still being used to encourage support for violent guerrilla movements and that a theological rationale has been developed for revolution which is comparable to the rationale developed by ministers and theological professors in the U.S. for support of World War II and the Korean War. In each case the rejection of an attempt at exact imitation of the life of Jesus is quite different from a rejection of the general life style of Jesus. Those who assert that Christ is "dynamic" and uses violence today are guilty of adapting him to their own political purposes. If Christ today differs substantially from the Jesus of the New Testament, so that

17. Discussion at which the author was present. Names are withheld to protect others who were present.

one acts contrary to the love revealed by the other, then Christ can become a tool of any right- or left-wing group that wants to use him, as North American clergymen have done in support of imperialist wars. Men are not liberated from oppressing when they are killed, unless we also acknowledge that the way to liberate the oppressed is by killing them.

Torres's most serious error was to have lent support to the idea that there is no distinctively Christian approach to oppression and violence that has not already been preempted by both the Left and the Right.

In fairness to Torres it should be noted that much of the attempt to use him as a symbol of violence came from others. The commanders of the ALN after his death issued a statement which said: "His remembrance has filled our hearts with fighting spirit and hatred for the mercenaries of the oligarchy. . . . Priests, take the martyrdom of Camilo as a sublime example of love of neighbors . . ."[18] Torres's brother Fernando issued a different sort of statement:

Camilo was a victim of the universal violence which is seen every day in the entire world and which has tormented Colombia for many years. Let us not allow the image of Camilo to be obscured by increasing that violence and the number of Colombian dead, using his name as a standard.[19]

Torres, unlike Che Guevara, was not primarily a man of violence. He was ambivalent, taking violence and also saying: "I do not want violence."[20]

It is doubtful if Torres could ever have become the hardened man of violence that Che became. It was Che who persuaded Castro "that a humanistic revolution is impossible in the twentieth century. 'In order to succeed and to last,' he told him, 'a revolution must put every aspect of the structure into question and create the irrevocable. It

18. Guzman, *Camilo Torres*, p. 254.
19. Ibid., p. 283.
20. Lartéguy, *The Guerrillas*, p. 130.

can therefore only be brutal, irreversible, and Marxist.' "[21]

Guevara was a Stalinist in ethics. What Torres would have become if he had lived through several years of warfare is difficult to say. We do know that in the case of both Che and Torres, their early deaths created myths and for millions have romanticized violence as the way to freedom. If they had continued to live and had continued to fail, they would not have become such heroic symbols. As it is, their deaths, which need not have occurred if they had shown political or military wisdom, have endowed them with a kind of revolutionary symbolism that others are supposed to emulate. Yet even this symbolism has not strengthened the guerrilla movement or demonstrated any success in the struggle for liberation or pointed any distinctively new directions for Latin Americans, who are desperately in need of ending the oppression of their own and North American structures of violence.

21. Ibid., pp. 43, 44.

8

COUP D'ÉTAT AND TYRANNICIDE

THE ASSUMPTION that an armed seizure of power is necessary for liberation has not only been central to revolutionary doctrine but has also been accepted by many who want to change a specific government. It has been idealized or romanticized in Christian thought by the acclaim given to Dietrich Bonhoeffer for his participation in the conspiracy to assassinate Adolf Hitler and launch a coup d'état which would give the army control over Germany. Bonhoeffer's role in the conspiracy was relatively minor. He was not a part of the military group who planned the assassination and coup. Neither did he personally attempt to kill Hitler. He has nevertheless become an important illustration and symbol for Protestant churchmen who want to justify violence or assassination. They refer to Bonhoeffer's actions as based on Christian love and therefore as an acceptable illustration if not a model for Christian conduct under certain circumstances.

Before examining the context of Bonhoeffer's action it may be useful to discuss briefly the coup d'état and assassination. The coup d'état is usually not intended as a prelude to revolution but as a means of transferring power from one ruling elite to another. It has been used, for example, to take power from a government that is adjudged as too reactionary or too liberal or too arbitrary. A coup can be bloodless, as evident in the use of overwhelming military strength at a crucial point. There have been instances of bloodless coups in Latin America when the armed forces decided to take over rule from a civilian-led government. However, coups often involve lethal violence either in the form of armed struggle or assassination or both.

There are three main objections to the coup. It is usually designed as a quick seizure of power at the seat of government to forestall the mobilization of any forces that might lead to civil war. Slight miscalculation, however, can lead to serious and destructive fighting that may engulf an entire nation. The coup also is designed to remove one or more men so as to improve the government. This is a possible outcome, but liberation, as distinct from improvement, requires systematic or structural change. The third objection is the precedent and even habit of overthrowing governments which are created by coups instead of encouraging governmental change by nonmilitary processes.

There are also objections to the assassination of rulers, including tyrants. The chief political objection to tyrannicide is that it may lead to martyrdom. The original meaning of the word *martyr* was "witness" and came from the Greek, *martus*. Any public figure who has some popular following represents some position, policy or stance that appeals to his supporters. His assassination, for whatever reason, is likely to be associated with what he and his followers believe. The killing of any except the most despicable of public figures seems to add an aura of rightness to their policies and even righteousness and greatness to them personally.

The motion picture, *Becket*, and the history of that time reveal that the martyrdom of Thomas à Becket established the political rightness of his position for centuries even though his position was subsequently overruled. He was made a saint by the Roman Catholic church in spite of the fact that he was a violent and self-centered man. Z. N. Brooke in an authoritative study writes of Becket, "He was so self centered that he would often sacrifice the prospect of an advantage in order to gain the ephemeral satisfaction of a verbal victory. As Archbishop, except perhaps at the very beginning and at the very end, there is little in him of the spiritually minded man."[1]

Becket was martyred in a conflict caused by Henry II who wanted the government to be able to try to settle criminal and property cases involving clerics and other church officers in civil rather than ecclesiastical courts. Becket, by means of his martyrdom, won with the result that it took almost seven hundred years to remove the "last remains of old powers of ecclesiastical jurisdiction in reference to secular cases" from the statute books.[2] If Becket had remained alive, it is by no means certain that he would have won even a short-term victory over Henry II, for he was very close to losing the struggle. T. S. Eliot in his *Murder in the Cathedral*, which deals with the assassination of Becket, has the Fourth Tempter say: "Saint and martyr rule from the tomb."

Martyrdom damages the cause of those who do the killing and improves the image of a public figure. John F. Kennedy, for example, was simply an average president who began the escalation of the war in Vietnam and was an imperialist abroad and as friendly to powerful corporations at home as any president. His assassination, however, began the Kennedy legend.

It is possible to speculate that the reason the British Empire did not kill Gandhi, as it did some other Indians

1. Z. N. Brooke, *The English Church and the Papacy* (Cambridge: Cambridge University Press, 1952), p. 211.
2. *Encyclopaedia Britannica*, 1962, s.v. "Ecclesiastical Jurisdiction."

involved in the struggle for India's freedom, was the fear of making him a martyr. The Nazi government in Germany similarly did not execute Martin Niemöller, though Hitler had some less well-known churchmen shot. One of those churchmen executed by the Hitler government was Dietrich Bonhoeffer, who was arrested and shot because of his part in a conspiracy to kill Adolf Hitler.

The attempted coup and assassination of Hitler during World War II are an interesting case study of the problems involved in such use of violence, especially in industrialized countries. The assumption of those involved in the coup was that Hitler's move to take Germany into war and his brutal liquidation of enemies in Germany and other countries was the result of one man's leadership and therefore could be modified or stopped if he were no longer in command of the government.

Hitler was obviously the leader of the Nazi movement and obviously a tyrant. Yet these facts in themselves might not justify tyrannicide. The concept of tyrannicide was given political value in primitive societies where the assassination of a despot was virtually certain to bring to power either a benevolent son or an impotent one with a more humane regent. But in more complex societies it is highly unlikely that the evils of any country can be traced solely to one person. The idea that there is a symbolic or actual devil whose removal would solve a given crisis or end oppression, totalitarianism, or war is a myth. There are always preconditions for oppression and totalitarianism. Dictators, for example, do not suddenly impose tyranny upon an unwilling people. "Hitler," according to Hans Frank at Nuremberg "was the Devil. Thus he led us all astray." To this a German writer replied that "a people must first be in a condition to be led astray before it can abandon itself to the totalitarian adventure."[3]

The rise of totalitarianism and of Adolf Hitler can be

3. Joachim C. Fest, *The Face of the Third Reich* (New York: Pantheon Books, 1970), p. 304.

traced to a number of factors, one of which was the importance and far-reaching influence of the military. All totalitarian societies are organized according to the military
principles of command and obedience, "leadership," and
discipline. During the "first Reich" when the kaiser ruled,
as over against the "second Reich" of the Weimar Republic, the German officer corps was in effect the sovereign
power.

In times of civil disturbance . . . the Kaiser could by a mere
stroke of the pen, invest it with the whole of the Civil authority
both judicial and executive, throughout the Reìch . . . in all
this dispersion of civil authority under the federal confederation
of the first Reich of the Kaiser, the one great instrument about
whose authority there could be no dispute was the Army and its
principals, the German Officers' Corps. It was an authority at
once overwhelming and penetrating, throwing its vast shadow
over the whole Reich and intruding into every one of the
constituent states from the North Sea to the Bavarian Alps. The
German Officers' Corps was the spear-point of Prussian hegemony throughout the Reich.[4]

During the Weimar Republic and the partial disarmament of Germany, the Officers' Corps maintained a hostile
neutrality or aloof disregard with respect to the civilian
administration and legislatures, but behind the scenes the
army steadily used its influence to change the political
situation that made the Weimar Republic possible.[5]

General von Einem, who had been minister of war,
stated in 1933:

I have hated the Social Democrats all my life. Until the present
day I have not been able to discover a single one of their ideas
which was not in principle somehow detrimental to State and

4. J. H. Morgan, *Assize of Arms: The Disarmament of Germany and Her Rearmament 1919–1939* (New York: Oxford
University Press, 1946), pp. 125, 126.
5. Hans Ernest Fried, *The Guilt of the German Army* (New
York: Macmillan, 1942), p. 78; H. Foertsch, *Die Wehrmacht
im Nationalsozialistischen Staat* (Hamburg, 1935), pp. 11, 17.

nation. I have waged the struggle against them with the purest conscience and from innermost conviction. . . .[6]

During the 1930s while President von Hindenburg was in office, the real power behind the president was General Kurt von Schleicher. He told the assembled army commanders of Germany in 1930

that among other groups, many people belonged to the Nazis from "circles which stand close to us;" the Nazis' foreign political programme, although not practicable at the moment, was, he said, welcome to the army, as was their fight against pernicious influences in the cultural and political life of Germany.[7]

In 1931, von Schleicher told Chancellor Heinrich Bruning that his government must develop more of an orientation to the Right if any real understanding between the government and the German Officers' Corps was to be maintained.[8] In 1932, von Schleicher played a leading role in intrigues which forced the resignation of Bruning and the selection of Franz von Papen as chancellor. After a few months General von Schleicher succeeded von Papen as chancellor. It was the Hitler–von Papen government that succeeded von Schleicher.

Thus, wrote a British historian, F. L. Carsten,

the army leaders, by their intrigues and their deep-rooted antipathy to parliamentary government, prepared the way, first for a series of non-parliamentary semi-dictatorial governments ruling through the authority of the President, and finally for an entirely despotic government, which destroyed the political parties, parliament and the constitution.[9]

6. von Einem, *Erinnerungen eines Soldaten* (Leipzig, 1933, p. 67) as quoted in F. L. Carsten, "From Scharnhorst to Schleicher: The Prussian Officer Corps in Politics, 1806–1933" in Michael Howard, ed., *Soldiers and Government* (London: Eyre and Spottiswoode, 1957), p. 82.

7. Ibid., p. 91.
8. Ibid., p. 92.
9. Ibid., p. 93.

National Socialism or the Nazi movement led by Adolf Hitler was the creature of German militarism, not its creator. Hans Ernest Fried wrote that National Socialism was in its earliest days "a tool of the most important faction among the high officers garrisoned in the capital of Bavaria" which was the second largest state in Germany. "From the very start the tiny National Socialist Party was backed and inspired by the highest military circles. . . ." Other similar movements were also backed but were less successful.[10]

The military and industrial supports for Hitler and his movement were numerous. Franz Seldte, the Magdeburg reserve officer and manufacturer who founded the *Stahlhelm* (Steel Helmet) in December 1918, was a member of the coalition cabinet formed on January 30, 1933, of which Hitler was the head. The *Stahlhelm*, which was the largest and most representative veterans organization in Germany, reliably reflected the ideas about military influence and patriotism of the officer and ex-officer class and was able to condition the political opinions of the civilian conservative and upper-middle classes. Field Marshal von Hindenburg, the president of the German Republic, was the honorary president of the *Stahlhelm* and the man who invited Hitler to serve as chancellor of the coalition government that led to the abolition of the democratic Weimar regime. Von Hindenburg, who was eighty-six and who reportedly had some doubts about Hitler, was under the influence of his son Major Oskar von Hindenburg and others who wanted Hitler as chancellor.

Hitler had previously surrounded himself with officers. In 1930, all of the high military commanders of his storm troopers were former career officers and three of these were also aristocrats. Captain Wilhelm Göring, who played an important role in the growth of the Nazi party, was the son of the former resident governor of the German colony

10. Fried, *German Army*, p. 20.

of Southwest Africa. General von Seeckt, the regular army commander who during the early days of the Republic had stood by while an armed band occupied Berlin and forced the government to flee, was elected to the Reichstag in 1930. Thereafter he allied himself openly with Hitler for a time and asked his sister in 1932 to vote for Hitler instead of for von Hindenburg as president.[11]

The Nazi movement not only spoke to the mood of the army but also to the needs of big business who wanted rearmament and military orders. The Nazis promised rearmament and also that the German people would be led away from socialism, communism, and the weaknesses of democracy. In the summer of 1931, Walther Funk, who was the editor of an important German financial paper, gave up his lucrative job to join the Nazi party and serve as the contact between certain key business leaders and the party. At the Nuremberg trials he stated that a number of his industrialist friends had asked him to become active in the Nazi party "in order to persuade the party to follow the course of private enterprise."[12]

Hitler met privately with influential business leaders so as not to let the people know that he was going to betray social democratic principles. Some of the industrialists who worked with Hitler were exposed at Nuremberg. They include: Fritz Thyssen, the head of the steel trust; Emil Kirdorf, a coal baron; Albert Voegler, an important figure in the United Steel Works; a number of leading bankers; George von Schnitzler of I. G. Farben; and others such as Hugo Bruckman, a wealthy Munich publisher.[13]

Hitler increased his military support after he became chancellor by launching a new, secret program for rearmament, by abolishing civil court jursidiction over the military, by crushing antiwar and antimilitarist movements,

11. William L. Shirer, *The Rise and Fall of the Third Reich* (New York: Fawcett World Library, 1962), pp. 200, 201.

12. Ibid., p. 201.

13. Ibid., p. 204.

and by various other measures. John Gunther wrote that

Rearmament was covert until October, 1933, when Germany left the League; an open secret until March, 1935, when Hitler tore up the military clauses of Versailles and introduced conscription; since March, 1935, the Reich has been an enormous military camp, with no falseface about it. And in March, 1936, the demilitarized Rhineland zone was occupied.[14]

The question was often asked, who is really the ruler in Germany, the army or Hitler? John Gunther in 1938 responded: "The fact is that both rule Germany. And so long as their aims are identical little chance of conflict between them exists. . . . Each needs the other."[15]

Hitler, however, needed to curry personal support from the army when a crisis in relationships occurred: The army went on alert and pressed for a purge of Hitler's storm troops (SA) which seemed to the Officers' Corps to be developing into a people's army. Hitler moved rapidly to kill Roehm, the SA head, and scores of other SA leaders. He also had military opponents killed, including General von Schleicher and General Kurt von Bredow. In spite of the murder of the two officers, the liquidation of Hitler's private S.A. produced the desired result. On July 2, President von Hindenburg thanked Hitler and a day later General von Blomberg, defense minister, legitimized the slaughter by congratulating Hitler and issuing an order of the day to the army indicating the army command's agreement with the events. In this action the army accepted Hitler's abandonment of law and order and approved of terrorism.[16] The Officers' Corps, however, publicly condemned the murder of General von Schleicher with the result that thereafter Hitler did not deal with high officers until after they were dismissed from the army.[17]

14. John Gunther, *Inside Europe* (New York: Harper and Brothers, 1938), p. 80.
15. Ibid., pp. 82, 83.
16. Shirer, *Third Reich*, pp. 304–13.
17. Morgan, *Disarmament of Germany*, p. 156.

Following the death of von Hindenburg, August 1, 1934, the army consented to Hitler's becoming both president and chancellor of Germany. Shortly thereafter he required that all officers and men in the armed forces take the following oath which bound them personally to him:

I swear by God this sacred oath, that I will render unconditional obedience to Adolf Hitler, the Fuehrer of the German Reich and people, Supreme Commander of the Armed Forces, and will be ready as a brave soldier to risk my life at any time for this oath.

The officers who could have overthrown the Hitler government were thereafter in the position of having to honor their oath or to violate it and thus also violate their code and honor as officers.

There were officers throughout the period of Hitler's planning and directing of war who disagreed with Hitler, some of whom entered conspiracies directed against him. But they were always either too few or not strategically located or else in doubt about their role. One German authority wrote of these dissident officers that their helplessness was partly due to the facing of a totalitarian regime but also to "the inner helplessness of a man caught up in the characteristic ideas of his caste. . . . Respect for the now purely formal authority of the oath of obedience remained insurmountable."[18]

Another reason for the early failure of the officers to resist Hitler was the rearmament of Germany. They were caught up in the feverish activity which also offered "accelerated promotion and a renewed sense of social importance."[19] Many of the officers who disliked the vulgarity and adventurism of the Nazis nevertheless believed they could be used to achieve rearmament and stronger national

18. Fest, *Third Reich*, p. 243.
19. Harold C. Deutsch, *The Conspiracy Against Hitler in the Twilight War* (Minneapolis: University of Minnesota Press, 1968), p. 26.

discipline before being ousted or that the Nazis would mellow and become more acceptable.

By the middle of 1938, a military opposition to Hitler had developed under the leadership of the chief of the general staff, Ludwig Beck. Beck, however, resigned in opposition to Hitler's demand for unconditional obedience with respect to his political decisions and especially over the proposed attack on Czechoslovakia. He remained, however, an important factor behind the scenes. Others in the opposition included Admiral Wilhelm Canaris, the head of the Abwehr (armed forces intelligence), his chief of staff, Colonel Hans Oster, and Beck's successor, General Holder. Oster and Beck worked out a plan to use both civilians and military personnel to arrest Hitler and kill him while resisting arrest. The commanders of the Berlin military district and the Potsdam area were ready with regiments to support the coup, the purpose of which was to prevent Hitler's launching a European war. Beck and Baron Ernst von Weizsacker, state secretary of the foreign office, sent representatives to London to tell of their plans and to express their concern about any policy that would encourage Hitler to take Czechoslovakia.

On two occasions in September 1938, the orders were given authorizing the coup for the following day, only to have them stopped by announcements of Prime Minister Neville Chamberlain's approaching visits to Germany. The Munich agreement and subsequent events gave Hitler such prestige that it would have been almost impossible for the opposition to Hitler to rally the nation against him.[20] The opposition therefore concentrated on persuading army generals to discourage Hitler from pressing for an attack on the West. They were successful and a number of generals tried but without success to discourage a proposed attack on Holland. One of the generals, Walter von Reichenau, suggested to the opposition leaders that they warn the British and Dutch of the plans, which they did.

20. Ibid., pp. 37, 38.

Once the German armies were successful against Poland and all of Western Europe it was much more difficult to get rid of Hitler. Few Germans would have understood in the midst of such victories that Hitler was leading them to the destruction the opposition or resistance leaders foresaw. The resistance leaders then concentrated on preparing for the "right psychological moment."[21]

After the German defeat at Stalingrad a number of officers, including Colonel Claus von Stauffenberg, the architect of the conspiracy to assassinate Hitler, became convinced that the war could not be won by military measures and must be ended by diplomatic methods.[22]

Attempts were made to establish contact with the British and Americans, with the pope in Rome, and with Protestant leaders in various countries. Dietrich Bonhoeffer was one of the persons the resistance sent to Norway, Sweden, Switzerland, and Rome under the protection of the Abwehr, ostensibly working for military intelligence. Bonhoeffer's friendship with Dr. George Bell, the bishop of Chichester, was used to get a message to Anthony Eden in the British Foreign Office. Anthony Eden's response was that the resistance movement in Germany must become active, for it had shown no obvious evidence that it existed.[23]

The various efforts by a number of Germans to make contact with the Western Allies were intended not only to inform them about the resistance but also to get some reply indicating that if Hitler were successfully eliminated, the Allies would not continue the war but give those who carried off the coup a chance to reorganize a peaceful Germany. Von Stauffenberg and his associates drew up an

21. Hans Rothfels, *The German Opposition to Hitler* (Chicago: Henry Regnery Company, 1962), p. 74.

22. Joachim Kramarz, *Stauffenberg: The Architect of the Famous July 20th Conspiracy to Assassinate Hitler* (New York: Macmillan, 1967), p. 112.

23. Rothfels, *German Opposition*, p. 137.

eleven point program to propose to the Allied Supreme Command, which provided that a Germany without Hitler would, in return for cancellation of Allied plans for the invasion of France and no occupation of Germany, agree to the following: Free elections for the new German government; withdrawal to the 1914 frontiers in the east; continuance of "Austria and the Sudetenland as an integral part of the Reich; autonomy for Alsace-Lorraine"; and German war criminals to be dealt with by Germany herself.[24] These were demands but were also understood as a basis for negotiation rather than a final position. There seems little doubt, however, that the conspirators were motivated by a concern for European civilization and by the religious traditions of Christianity rather than simply by German nationalism.

The Allies, however, insisted on unconditional surrender and would not negotiate. Allen Dulles, the head of American intelligence in Europe, said that "the conspirators were told that they could count on no promises of any kind on the part of the Allies, but that if they were prepared to do so, they would have to go ahead, not in the hope of better peace terms, but simply because their duty to put their own house in order was an absolute one."[25]

There were various reasons for the conspirators' inability to get much support from the leading generals even after various reverses had begun. One was their unwillingness to move against Hitler without Allied assurances. Another was the fear that an attempt on Hitler's life might lead to the collapse of the German government and a Communist conquest of all Europe.[26] Still other generals felt they could do nothing against Hitler because their troops could not be counted on under those circumstances.[27]

In spite of the refusal of the bulk of the generals to sup-

24. Kramarz, *Stauffenberg*, pp. 166, 167.
25. Rothfels, *German Opposition*, p. 151.
26. Ibid., p. 831; Kramarz, *Stauffenberg*, p. 110.
27. Deutsch, *Conspiracy Against Hitler*, p. 256.

port a coup there were several attempts at assassination by lower-ranking officers with the one on July 20, 1944, costing the lives of most of the conspirators. The July 20 attempt also involved the use of German army regiments to take control of the government. Some of these moved on schedule but the coup was defeated largely through faulty planning and the dependence on Hitler's death from a planted bomb.

The entire conspiracy was based on the assumption that a coup would restore Germany to a government acceptable to the German army's general staff and that such a government would be acceptable to the Western Allies. The government would be elected as had others in the past, but the officers who permitted or carried out the coup would have had to carry out the election. The conspiracy was not based simply on the assassination of Hitler because the army officers were not prepared to have Hitler's successors in the Nazi party carry on the war.

Given this background, Bonhoeffer's participation in the conspiracy raises many questions about his political judgment. Was he really so naïve as to believe that Hitler's assassination before Germany's defeat would change the people and the army to such an extent that they would abandon the militarism, nationalism, rabid anticommunism and anti-Semitism that had made the rise of nazism possible? Did he really believe that the few dedicated officers in the conspiracy were representative of the whole officer class and would themselves depart from tradition to set up an antimilitarist government following the coup? Or did he believe Hitler was the devil incarnate whose death would simply permit the forces of good to triumph?

Such questioning of Bonhoeffer's political judgment is not intended as an indictment of his good intentions or his courage; neither does it derogate his valuable contributions to theological and ethical thought. Although Bonhoeffer is significant as a theologian, there is little doubt that it is his political activity and death at the hands of the Hitler government which have made his name so widely known. The comments that follow are therefore directed at his political judgment and at the Christian romanticism that uses him as a model for Christian justification of violence.

Bonhoeffer's naïvete politically was demonstrated in the 1930s in believing as Eberhard Bethge, the friend and biographer of Bonhoeffer, asserts he did, that "the beginning of the war would bring about the final catastrophe for Hitler."[28] Bethge rightly indicated that the civilian opponents of Hitler could not win much support from the generals while they were successful and when there was little military reason to question their oath to obey Hitler.[29] On another occasion, in spite of the way the German army accepted Hitler's terrorism against Germans, Bonhoeffer was optimistic that German commanders would not liquidate Russian civilians and military personnel as Hitler had ordered and would because of such orders be encouraged to resist Hitler.[30] Yet they did carry out Hitler's orders.

If Bonhoeffer and the others who opposed Hitler could not arrange a coup d'état while the German armies were winning, it was certainly foolish to believe as Bonhoeffer did that the Allies would be willing to stop the war after they began to win. They would in that event have had to allow German generals who had not opposed Hitler's destruction of the Weimar Republic to govern Germany.

In fact the German generals involved in the conspiracy were not prepared to run serious risks without an Allied guarantee that Germany would not be disarmed and that they would be allowed to set up a government different from nazism. Bonhoeffer wrote: ". . . the question must be faced whether a German government which makes a complete break with Hitler and all he stands for can hope to get such terms of peace that it has some chance to survive. . . . It is clear that the answering of this question is a

28. Eberhard Bethge, *Dietrich Bonhoeffer* (New York: Harper and Row, 1970), p. 568.
29. Ibid.
30. Ibid., p. 636, 637.

matter of urgency, since the attitude of opposition groups in Germany depends upon the answer given. . . ."[31]

One might well question Bonhoeffer's judgment in allying himself with a group that would function only if Germany were given guarantees of peace without too much loss. The best response is that he had to work with the only group that was able to offer any hope, once he had committed himself to the idea that the violent destruction of Hitler was the goal to which he was called.

Bonhoeffer's role in the conspiracy was to get assurance from the British government through his ecumenical church contacts that in the event of a revolt against Hitler the British and other military commanders would suspend operations, forego any attack during the revolt and clearing up process, and give the new government enough time to get properly underway.[32]

Bonhoeffer knew so little of political reality that he assumed the British, Russian, and American governments would give up victory to let an unproven group of men govern Germany. The whole history of British-French-American world dominance during and following the Versailles treaty did not predispose Churchill and Roosevelt (to say nothing about Stalin) to give Germany a chance to continue as an undefeated power in Europe simply because of the elimination of Hitler. There is some evidence that Bonhoeffer believed the Allies might want guarantees against the return of National Socialism and might also want to establish military safeguards, but he apparently believed that the Allies were solely interested in a peaceful Germany rather than in all the efforts toward business penetration of Europe and worldwide political hegemony that were implicit in the nature of the American colossus and the British Empire.[33]

31. Ibid., p. 645.

32. Ibid., p. 662.

33. John M. Swomley, Jr., *American Empire* (New York: Macmillan, 1970), chap. 6.

As indicated earlier, Anthony Eden in June 1942, apparently received word about the group of conspirators and their desire for assurance, but after contacts with the Americans and the Russians, the decision was against any action such as the German generals wanted. Thereafter the Germans who wanted a coup operated on the assumption that if it were successful it might receive the support of the German people and some modification by the Allies of their demand for unconditional surrender.[34]

Bonhoeffer was mistaken at still other points. He believed that the churches' political views were taken seriously by the war-making governments. Insofar as church spokesmen, like Reinhold Niebuhr in the United States, endorsed the war aims of the government, they were honored by those in key political positions. But Bonhoeffer assumed that prominent churchmen in Europe and England who were his friends could sell the British government on the goals of the German military leaders with whom Bonhoeffer had allied himself. Bonhoeffer, for example, expressed surprise that the British Broadcasting Corporation said nothing in its broadcasts "about the [British] churches' great discussion of the new order" which it might have used as propaganda directed toward building the German resistance movement, especially toward the generals who were still indecisive.[35] The Anglican bishop of Chichester, George Bell, did try to persuade his contacts in the British cabinet that Bonhoeffer had carried word about "peace-proposals" from some German military leaders but Bell acknowledged that his case was weak given the fact that there was no visible evidence of a revolt against Hitler.[36]

A more serious question relates to overall political analysis. The conspirators from the beginning—even be-

34. William Kuhns, *In Pursuit of Dietrich Bonhoeffer* (Dayton: Pfloum Press, 1967), p. 114.
35. Bethge, *Bonhoeffer*, p. 644.
36. Ibid., pp. 670, 671.

fore the war—apparently believed that the elimination of Hitler would solve their problem. They did not seem to realize that there was more to the German problem than the uniqueness of Hitler. Hitler was not simply a conqueror of German public opinion and of army loyalty but an answer to what millions of Germans, especially the army had wanted. To believe that the evil forces in Germany such as anti-Semitism, militarism, nationalism, a desire for order at the expense of freedom, the cheapness of human life, and other evidences of the totalitarian mind would disappear with Hitler was wishful thinking. It is not quite tantamount to saying that the assassination of Lyndon Johnson would have ended the war in Vietnam but is more a parallel with the idea that the assassination of a racist governor in Mississippi or Alabama between 1945 and 1965 would have changed the racial pattern in those states.

There was of course not just a series of mistakes in political analysis but an acute ignorance of the danger of martyrdom. At almost any stage in Hitler's rule of Germany, except possibly after his defeat, his assassination would probably have resulted in martyrdom. There was an incident during the war which some believe was engineered by the government to build enthusiasm for the war. A young man, George Elser, was arrested in Munich for attempting to kill Hitler.[37]

In any event there was some consideration given by those around Bonhoeffer as to the danger of martyring Hitler. Bishop George Bell wrote in 1945:

We know of a meeting held at that time where it was proposed that further action should be postponed so as to avoid giving Hitler the character of a martyr if he should be killed. Bonhoeffer's rejoinder was decisive: "If we claim to be Christian, there is no room for expediency. Hitler is the Antichrist. Therefore

37. Mary Bosanquet, *The Life and Death of Dietrich Bonhoeffer* (London: Hodder and Stoughton, 1968), p. 223.

we must go on with our work and eliminate him whether he be successful or not."[38]

Bethge thinks that Bonhoeffer did not really believe Hitler was the Antichrist. That particular term, however, is irrelevant to the question of martyrdom; for Bethge rightly asserts that after Hitler's tremendous military success anyone who succeeded in killing Hitler would be responsible for another "stab-in-the-back" legend such as Generals Ludendorf and von Hindenburg created after World War I.[39] Yet Bonhoeffer is clearly reported as pleading for Hitler's assassination. He had been to Norway in April 1942, with Helmuth von Moltke, to encourage the resistance of the pastors and teachers against Quisling's rule. In their discussions von Moltke was reported as having refused to participate in an attempt to eliminate Hitler by violence whereas Bonhoeffer felt it was necessary.[40]

Bethge wrote that "Bonhoeffer's position in the Resistance Movement was of no great importance politically, and he himself did not overrate his place and his professional competence in that respect."[41] His political significance, however, arises partly from his own martyrdom, partly from the fact that he was a churchman who acted on his convictions, but chiefly for another reason: he has become the symbol of Christian intellectual validation of the use of assassination and of violent revolutionary activity. This political significance, as has been suggested, is not the result of political astuteness or of sound political analyses but of a romantic belief that assassination of tyrants is somehow more effective or more loving than other types of resistance.

Bonhoeffer to some degree encouraged the idea that his actions were responsible and a useful pattern for future generations, though most of his elevation as an example

38. Bethge, *Bonhoeffer*, pp. 626, 627.
39. Ibid., pp. 627, 628.
40. Ibid., p. 659.
41. Ibid., p. 700.

arises from the desire of armchair theologians to find a Christian model and theological rationale for their position of violent revolution.

In a familiar passage Bonhoeffer writes of "the man of freedom" as one "who values the necessary deed more highly than a clear conscience or the duties of his calling, who is ready to sacrifice a barren principle for a fruitful compromise or a barren mediocrity for a fruitful radicalism."[42]

This suggests that neither conscience nor principle are reliable guides to action. But that kind of a generalization could only refer to someone who had a poorly formed conscience or inadequate principle. Bonhoeffer, however, didn't mean any of these, for he explains in the same context that he is speaking of "the man whose ultimate criterion is not his reason, his principle, his conscience, his freedom or his virtue but who is ready to sacrifice all these things when he is called to obedient and responsible action in faith and exclusive allegiance to God."[43]

This is a curious rationale for his actions, written from prison. He says that the call of God is beyond reason or principle, beyond conscience or virtue and yet is a call to responsible action. This is precisely where Bonhoeffer's rationalization of his action is most questionable—to assume that God called him to participate in the assassination of a tyrant in spite of any reason, principles, or conscience to the contrary. Faith is not to be equated with any or every kind of action against evil. To assert that God demands a disregard of reason and conscience and principle is to assume that these are invalid guides under normal circumstances or that God makes use of them normally but not in unusual circumstances. The test of Bonhoeffer's action of course lies in its failure. Either God did not really

42. Dietrich Bonhoeffer, *Prisoner for God*, ed. Eberhard Bethge, trans. Reginald H. Fuller (New York: Macmillan, 1960), p. 15.
43. Ibid., pp. 15, 16.

call Bonhoeffer to act in spite of a reasonable political analysis of the situation, or else God was powerless to assist in the enterprise of saving Germany through a different set of generals. It is of course no answer to say that Bonhoeffer will be remembered as a symbol of Christian resistance to Hitler, whereas the man he sought to assassinate will be remembered as diabolical. Hitler's name would have been a name of infamy whether Bonhoeffer had ever existed. And resistance to Hitler in the person of church leaders will be remembered in the names of Martin Niemöller and Karl Barth who were far greater symbols during the war than was Bonhoeffer. Bonhoeffer, of necessity, worked secretly, whereas the defiance of Niemöller and hundreds of others was open. Bonhoeffer took risks but hoped that his alliance with certain military leaders plus the secrecy of his work would help him avoid detection. Those who openly resisted the Nazi movement had no such relative protection and were actually therefore more valuable symbols of church resistance to totalitarianism during the war itself. They did not maintain a façade of support but were effective symbols precisely because they stood their ground on the basis of reason, conscience, and principles which thousands of clergymen and laymen could understand at the moment.

Why is it necessary to write these words about Bonhoeffer and the German situation almost thirty years following the war? The reason is that the martyrdom of Bonhoeffer, as is very often the case with martyrs, has led to a type of romanticism which exalts not simply the man but the idea of tyrannicide, conspiracy to plan coups d'état, and violent revolution, as if any one of these is the way, the truth, and the life when faced with tyranny and oppression. There is no intent to derogate the courage or the devotion of Bonhoeffer either to Germany or to God. Bonhoeffer himself has suggested that he acted not as a hero in face of certain defeat but as a "man of responsibilities" who was primarily concerned with "How is the coming generation to live?"

He answers the question as he did for himself by choosing to act on the basis of "concrete responsibility" rather than "abstract principle."[44] But this is not the real issue. Were Martin Niemöller and hundreds of others who resisted Hitler acting on the basis of abstract principle or concrete responsibility? The issue is the efficacy of encouraging "the coming generation" to believe that responsibility means the abandonment of reason and principle in order to use violence responsibly.

Bonhoeffer himself cast doubt on making a principle of violence as the most responsible course of action. In a brief discussion of "folly" he wrote:

On closer inspection it would seem that any violent revolution, whether political or religious, produces an outburst of folly in a large part of mankind. Indeed it would seem to be almost a law of psychology and sociology. The power of one needs the folly of the other. . . . the upsurge of power is so terrific that it deprives men of an independent judgment, and they give up trying—more or less unconsciously—to assess the new state of affairs for themselves.[45]

Bonhoeffer also cast doubt on the secret or conspiratorial mode of living when he wrote:

We have learnt the art of deception and of equivocal speech. Experience has made us suspicious of others, and prevented us from being open and frank. . . . Are we still serviceable? It is not the genius that we shall need, not the cynic, not the misanthropist, not the adroit tactician but honest, straightforward men. Will our spiritual reserves prove adequate and our candour with ourselves remorseless enough to enable us to find our way back again to simplicity and straightforwardness?[46]

This is one of the basic issues in all acts of deception and violence: whether the action conditions those who participate in it. Another basic issue is whether the elimination of a Hitler will eliminate nazism.

44. Ibid., pp. 17, 18.
45. Ibid., pp. 18, 19.
46. Ibid., p. 24.

9

HAZARDS OF VIOLENCE

THERE ARE at least five reasons for rejecting violence in favor of nonviolent action as a method of revolution today. The emphasis is on the word *today* because there is no point in insisting that violent revolution in a nonindustrialized world faced the same problems as it does in an industrial society.

1. The established order has a monopoly on the major weapons of violence and the means of detection, including wiretapping, electronic eavesdropping, accoustical sensors, etc. Any armed group that uses violence against the disciplined military forces of a modern industrial nation is always in danger of being wiped out.

2. Violent revolution implies the willingness to destroy anything in the old order that stands in the way of winning. Violence is not necessarily concerned with preserving the values of the past. Nonviolent revolution on the other hand is more likely to conserve the assets of the past while bringing in a new order. Nonviolent resistance "usually permits a large part of the agricultural and industrial work

of the people to go on and hence the life of the country can be maintained during the struggle."[1]

3. Violent revolution cannot be controlled by those who set it in motion. They cannot, for example, control the violence of the police and the military. If their violence escalates, an escalating rather than moderating response on the part of the revolutionaries is bound to occur. When both sides are committed to the use of violence, the more humane group must abandon its humaneness if it is to keep pace with the escalating violence and thus avoid losing. It is even possible that a revolutionary group could so force the pace of violence that a counterrevolutionary group or government in possession of nuclear weapons would use them rather than risk defeat at the hands of the insurgents.

4. The modern revolutionary purpose is negated by violence. That revolutionary purpose holds that human life is more important than possessions or power or anything else. All politics and all economics should be directed toward the liberation of men and women so they can find their highest good. Yet violent revolution asserts that the aims of the revolution are more important than the persons it is designed to benefit.

5. If the revolution is intended to eliminate the overt and covert violence which characterizes the existing order or structures of society, it can do so only by providing a nonviolent alternative structure for fulfilling the necessary function of the old order. It is unlikely that a revolutionary movement based on violence will, at the peak of armed might renounce the methods that brought it to power. The maintenance of the instruments of violence by any ruling group presupposes their use against another group and hence the maintenance of a system of oppression. This is evident in the fact that those who espouse violent revolu-

1. Richard Gregg, *The Power of Nonviolence* (Nyack, N.Y.: Fellowship Publications, 1959), p. 100.

tion concentrate their attack on men in power rather than on the concept and systems of state power. They do not plan to eliminate the army or the secret police or the myths of nationalism if they are successful in seizing power because they believe that their own control of the government ultimately depends on such systems which they can use to maintain control.

Violence even in a nonrevolutionary context tends to provoke violence in return. Overt violence provokes the more open or obvious violence. The Detroit Riot of 1943 which occurred in a crucial war situation did not impel the city of Detroit or the state of Michigan to solve the problems that caused it. Instead white reaction was built up that has never really subsided. Alfred McClung Lee, chairman of the Department of Sociology, Wayne State University, Detroit, and a colleague, Norman D. Humphrey, made a thorough study of the violence and concluded that the violence caused "an intensification of the feelings of individual insecurity, especially as expressed in fear and distrust of Negroes by whites and of whites by Negroes [as well as] the sudden growth of a kind of social paralysis—a tightening of the automatic controls exercised by society over its members, until these controls suppress any change whatever and all constructive social policies."[2]

More than twenty years later, following another riot in Detroit, the *Inner City Voice—Detroit's Black Community Newspaper* of March 23, 1968 said:

The thorough whipping we gave the power structure failed to open the eyes of most of the dumb honkies around Detroit. Instead of realizing that a new day is dawning in which the black man is going to be liberated, whole sections of Whiteyville decided they were going to fight to the death rather than see black people free. . . . Gun sales have jumped from 500 a month before the rebellion to 3,000 a week now. The majority of these weapons are in the hands of honkies.

2. Alfred McClung Lee and Norman D. Humphrey, *Race Riot* (New York: Octagon Press, 1968), pp. 85, 86.

White vigilante groups are being formed all over the suburban areas. In Macomb County many signs have been posted which read, Warning to Black Power—this area protected by citizens' militia.

The same paper reported that "immediately after the uprising" an organization called "Breakthrough" held a series of rallies in all white areas around Detroit. Each of these rallies was attended by an average of "4,000 honkies." The purpose was to "arm themselves, store supplies and organize into defense committees."

Eric Fromm, a distinguished psychiatrist, speaks of such "reactive violence" as arising when "people feel threatened and in order to defend themselves are willing to kill and destroy." He also speaks of "revengeful violence" and asserts that "the lower middle class, which are those most deprived in industrialized nations are . . . the focus of revenge feelings, just as they are the focus of racialist and nationalist feelings."[3]

The use of nonviolent action against an oppressive system may also provoke reprisal except in the case of a boycott. In a boycott it is always difficult to determine who is withholding purchasing power for political purpose and who does so for other reasons. Nevertheless the probability of violence being used against noncooperators led Gandhi, Martin Luther King, Jr., and others to emphasize the acceptance of suffering rather than the inflicting of it. They knew that if violence provoked those engaged in noncooperation also to use violence it would add another dimension to the problem and destroy the moral value and strategic purposes of the noncooperation. Violence arouses opposition to a movement by many persons who might otherwise have remained quiescent or acquiescent. Georges Sorel, who Mussolini said "contributed most" to the development of fascist "discipline, energy and power," wrote: "Every-

3. Eric Fromm, "Different Forms of Violence," *Fellowship*, March 1965, p. 5.

thing may be saved, if the proletariat by their use of violence, manage to re-establish the division into classes, and so restore to the middle class something of the former energy. . . ."[4] Sorel pointed out that when there is no real threat of overt violence there is a likelihood that the middle classes will be interested in "moderating disputes." He calls this tendency to preserve social peace "intermingling in the democratic marsh."[5] But if revolutionary violence can be provoked, those who previously wanted social peace can be stirred to aggressive action against the revolutionary elements. The major theorists of nonviolent direct action have also recognized that many people who are neither actively on the Right or the Left are aroused by violence from their ambivalence, or lethargy, or devotion to orderly change, because the violence which at the moment is directed against others may soon be directed at them.

Leaders of nonviolent campaigns count the beginning of violence by their followers as the beginning of the loss of the struggle because it shifts the problem from a moral and political conflict to a military one. In violent struggles on the other hand, there is often as much moral power in defending valued persons and ideas as in attacking them because they thwart social change. The task of the nonviolent revolutionary is to retain moral power by destroying evil systems without injuring those who are identified with those systems. There is both a pragmatic and a moral basis for wanting to convince opponents that their physical safety is not at stake. The pragmatic purpose is to concentrate their attention on the system and its evils rather than on their own physical defense. They are encouraged by the suffering of the noncooperators to realize that they share responsibility for the systemic violence as well as for the overt violence by the police. The moral purpose is to enhance respect for human life by not violating it.

4. Georges Sorel, *Reflections on Violence* (New York: Collier Books, 1961), pp. 24, 92.
5. Ibid., p. 92.

In all nonviolent direct action or noncooperation there are elements of coercion, persuasion, and acceptance or willingness to accept suffering. The intention of the coercion is not to break the opponent's will as violence does but to alter it by destroying his confidence and enthusiasm in the system he is defending. The fact of nonviolence permits negotiation and persuasion to continue during the conflict. The intention here is to persuade the opponent and at the same time permit him to demonstrate the rightness of his position if he can. The suffering is intended to win the sympathy and support of those who are sensitive to human suffering or who are similarly situated, as workers in one union are to members of another striking union. It also tends to demoralize the opponents who think of conflict in terms of violence. The demoralization is a result of finding themselves using violence against people who don't treat them as enemies or use violence in return. The chief reason for accepting rather than inflicting suffering is not based on a romantic notion that opponents will inevitably respond to the suffering of those who are nonviolent, but on a recognition that the inflicting of suffering is dehumanizing to those who do the injuring and killing. There is the conviction that liberation from dehumanizing systems is unlikely to be achieved by a process that is itself dehumanizing.

If it is argued that those who are most oppressed should not be asked to accept even more injury than is already their lot, one response is that they will have no security or freedom from hurt by *any* method of struggle for liberation. But it is also true that the oppressed who use nonviolent resistance are less likely to be killed or seriously injured. Richard Gregg, who spent a number of years in India and who worked with Gandhi for a time, wrote:

In the Indian struggle for independence . . . hundreds of thousands of Indians went to jail, probably not more than five hundred received permanent physical injuries, and probably not over eight thousand were killed immediately or died later from wounds. No British, I believe, were killed or wounded. Considering the importance and size of the conflict and the many years it lasted, these numbers are much smaller than they would have been if the Indians had used violence toward the British.[6]

Many more people were killed by the British in the shorter but violent struggle over Kenya and by the French in the Algerian Revolution and the United States in Vietnam. During the nonviolent civil-rights campaigns in the southern states more than fifty thousand persons were jailed but probably fewer than a hundred persons who engaged in those campaigns were killed.

The fundamental basis for the use of nonviolence in Martin Luther King's mind was pragmatic and at the same time theological. He did not view his practice as divorced from his theory about the universe. He believed in "the ultimate morality of the universe and . . . that all reality hinges on moral foundations."[7] Therefore any movement that would be truly liberating had to have a moral base which he affirmed as "the sacredness of all human life. Everyman is somebody because he is a child of God."[8]

The term *nonviolence* as used by both Gandhi and Martin Luther King was not the mere absence of violence, but shorthand for the social and economic power of noncooperation, plus the moral power of voluntary suffering for others. It assumed (1) that there is power in withdrawing support from evil or exploiting structure; (2) that opponents are human beings like themselves, to be respected and not violated; and (3) that the acceptance of suffering, rather than inflicting it on others, is itself a form of power, demoralizing to those who use violence without experiencing it in return and troublesome to the consciences of those who do not have an obvious vested interest in the maintenance of the system under attack.

6. Richard Gregg, *Non Violence*, p. 100.
7. Martin Luther King, Jr., *The Trumpet of Conscience* (New York: Harper and Row, 1967), p. 75.
8. Ibid., p. 72.

Both Gandhi and King understood that they were opposing systemic violence as well as the overt violence used in
crisis to defend the system. Their struggle was against violence as such and therefore could not succeed by their
endorsement or use of violence. Nonviolence as they used
it was not another method of in-fighting of one ideological
group against another, but a method of achieving reconciliation of adversaries together with the elimination or transformation of oppressive social structures. Much of modern
social and political action and all organized violence is
ideological in-fighting and counterproductive. The right
wing reinforces the left and vice-versa, so that instead of
changing systems fundamentally they periodically reinforce
each other. The Gandhi–King method, on the other hand,
was aimed at changing the system with the consent of at
least a proportion of those who were supporters of the
system. That method, developed by Gandhi, can be described dialectically. The purpose of nonviolence is to
bring opposing groups to a position "which is satisfactory
to both the original opposing antagonists, but in such a
way as to present an entirely new total circumstance."[9]
Those who use this Gandhian approach are "not seeking a
one sided triumph" but want to encourage "the best re-
structuring of the situation." They seek a victory, not over
the opponent "but over the system so as best to meet the
total human needs. . . ." This is a synthesis rather than a
compromise.[10] This approach is what led Dr. King to say:
"We have no desire to triumph over the white man and we
seek no such victory. When segregation on the buses is
ended, this will not be a victory for the Negro over the
white man, but of justice over injustice. And it will be a
victory for the best interests of the white people as well."

The question of ends and means inevitably arises in any
discussion of violence. Are people killed in order that peo-

9. Joan V. Bondurant, *Conquest of Violence* (Princeton,
N.J.: Princeton University Press, 1958), p. 195.
10. Ibid., p. 196.

ple may live? Are they imprisoned in order that they may be free? When persons are treated as means to a revolutionary goal instead of as ends in themselves, they are treated as objects to be used rather than as respected equals. No one is immune from his own dehumanizing acts. The taking of one life after another or the torture and terrorizing of one person after another has its effect on the one who engages in such acts. He has learned to view the life of his opponents as cheap. He may become calloused—a person who is sensitive to human need can participate in injuring and killing others only by hardening himself. Not all revolutionaries, however, are gentle people who develop calloused attitudes toward enemy humans. There are many who want to "get even" and some who enjoy hurting others. It is never possible in advance to be sure what will happen when persons with pent-up hatreds mingle in revolutionary forces with those who have tried to avoid hatred by hardening themselves to view human destruction as necessary.

Still another process takes place in the preparation for and the use of revolutionary violence. This is the attribution of overwhelming evil to the enemy. Unless the enemy becomes to some degree the Devil whose eradication will leave only the Good in unrivaled control, there is little point to the revolution. This means that the enemy is not a fellow human being but is distorted into an agent of evil. Berdyaev wrote:

If a man is possessed by the idea that all the evil in the world is to be found in the Jews or in the Masons or the bolshevists, in the heretics or in the bourgeoisie (and these not the real people but an idea of them invented by the imagination) then the best of men will be turned into a wild beast. This is a remarkable instance of human slavery.[11]

It is not just personal hardening or dehumanization that

11. Nicholas Berdyaev, *Slavery and Freedom* (London: Geoffrey Bles Centenary Press, 1943), p. 194.

occurs in an armed revolution. Society itself is changed when we violate the values we intend to conserve or promote. Nowhere has this been more apparent than in the Christian church and the institutions it has nurtured which, in the composite, have been called Christendom or "Christian" nations. The church turned away from an early concern about enemies and from a respect for human life to bless and support war for its own institutional purposes. The church not only identified itself with war-making states but with violence as such. The church led military crusades against non-Christians. Churches and their leaders engaged in warfare against rival church communities who interpreted Christianity in ways different from their own. They supported wars to maintain and to oppose human slavery. They supported wars to build and to destroy empires. For many years military chaplains assigned by the churches also have served as morale officers in the United States army.

If we look at violence historically, it is clear that the concept of a "just war" and of a "just revolution" originate in Christian rather than Marxist thought. The formulators and proponents of "just war" rules gave religious sanction to mass violence by supporting war on the false assumption that their rules would impose some restraints upon it. The just revolution can be traced to French Calvinist works such as the *Vindiciae contra tyrannos* published in 1579 which systematized the arguments for overthrowing tyrants, especially if they were of a contrary faith.[12]

It is not surprising that Christians who have advocated violence against the Germans or Japanese for threatening the economic or strategic interests of Americans should advocate violence against their fellow Americans and fellow Christians because they seek drastic social change or because they use disruptive tactics to stop the war in Vietnam. The Christian belief in violence is so great that

12. This was reprinted in London in 1924 with an introduction by Harold J. Laski, *A Defense of Liberty Against Tyrants.*

some Christians who want rapid social change also advocate revolutionary violence, if necessary, against their fellow Christians. A prominent professor of Christian ethics in a Protestant theological seminary indicated that he could not oppose violence against domestic injustice when he had supported armed violence during World War II and the Korean War.

The National Council of Churches of Christ in the United States, in a policy statement on violence, said that violent acts of revolution may be justifiable "when justice cannot be secured by any other means." Since there were no guidelines for determining when it is impossible to achieve justice by nonviolent processes, each individual would decide for himself which acts of destruction to commit—whether involving only property or also persons. One news commentator noted that "the Council statement was issued shortly after Senator Robert F. Kennedy was assassinated by a gunman who may well have believed that he was resisting injustice by the only effective means available to him."

The Christian acceptance of violence as the way to get "Christian" tasks done when some other method fails or seems to fail has had a profound impact on social values. If the community devoted to God, to salvation, to moral behavior, believes violence is an acceptable and even necessary form of fighting oppression or threatened conquest, why should non-Christians be blamed for following that example? Ironically, many modern Christians who have guns in their possession blame Marx or Lenin or Mao or others for spreading the idea of revolutionary violence, when it is the Christian West that is historically responsible both for overt and structural violence in the last fifteen hundred years. The Christian experience with violence should be a lesson to those who want to change the system by violence. Even with a good beginning such as Jesus and the early Christians gave the church, social values became corrupted when violence was used against persons, and human beings became a means to an end rather than valued as ends in themselves.

If violence tends to beget violence and if it also corrupts or hardens those who use it, are there ever occasions when violence may be used? We cannot be dogmatic in saying that any violence will destroy a revolution. Certainly violence which is isolated or incidental is different from the use of violence as the main thrust of revolutionary struggle. Yet it is also true that news media and the government itself tend to focus on any violence in an effort to discredit the whole resistance process. Martin Oppenheimer in his book, *The Urban Guerrilla*, indicates that "if a movement is not explicitly non-violent, it will be treated as if it were the most violent part."[13] This plus the fact that a failure to repudiate violent action might tolerate its increase is what led Gandhi to call off one of his campaigns when some of his followers engaged in violence.

Unfortunately many people do not think in terms of the best tactics to use in a given campaign. They do not analyze the consequences of violence. There is a tendency to do to others as they have done to you instead of doing to them what you wish they would do to you. Malcolm X illustrated this in the following:

. . . you should never be nonviolent unless you run into some nonviolence. I'm nonviolent with those who are nonviolent with me. But when you drop that violence on me, then you've made me go insane, and I'm not responsible for what I do. And that's the way every Negro should get. Anytime you know you're within the law, within your legal rights, within your moral rights, in accord with justice, then die for what you believe in. But don't die alone. Let your dying be reciprocal. This is what is meant by equality. What's good for the goose is good for the gander.[14]

13. Martin Oppenheimer, *The Urban Guerrilla* (Chicago: Quadrangle Books, 1969), p. 31.

14. Malcolm X, "The Ballot or the Bullet" in Herbert J. Storing, ed., *What Country Have I?* (New York: St. Martin's Press, 1970), p. 155.

This is an understandable statement on a level with those made by some Christians, both black and white, who are also moved by an emotional need to retaliate. But reciprocal action or responding in kind is not a strategy for dealing with the structures of oppression, which are enslaving to many whites as they are to blacks. The economic power structure tends to maintain unthreatened power by dividing the poor so that poor people find other poor people as a threat. Even if this is not a conscious strategy of the power elite, it is a fact that if unskilled or semi-skilled jobs are limited, only a limited number of the poor can find work. Partly for this reason, white ethnic minorities see black people as their enemies more than they do powerful whites who are unwilling to share their power. There is no point to violence which further alienates those whose cooperation against the power structure is sooner or later going to be necessary. The police, for example, are generally drawn from the white lower- and lower-middle classes. They do not make the decisions to gerrymander election districts so as to favor white candidates nor do they make the bank decisions which deny mortgage financing to black people. As some Black Panthers have put it, the police are not the enemy, they are tools of the enemy. David Dellinger rightly pointed out that "we must make a distinction, both philosophical and tactical, between institutions and the people who have been misled into serving them. . . . The unthinking revolutionist is misled by the crudity of the action that police and soldiers can be conditioned into performing." Minority revolutionary movements must seek to neutralize or to win their adversaries. They must also work to build alliances with those whose basic economic and political interests are identical.

The question as to what constitutes violence has been raised by the destruction of private and government property during the course of the Vietnam war. This question is of fundamental importance in any consideration of tactics.

Property is, of course, inanimate and therefore different

from living beings. Few would deny that the destruction of property is morally different from the killing of persons. Yet some property is an extension of personality in that it is necessary for the survival or well-being of a given person or group. The destruction of a family's rice paddy in Vietnam or a small city grocery store in which a family's lifetime of work has been invested is an example of property as the extension of personality. So also is a black man's home which for thirty or forty years he has labored to buy. No one who has seen a sixty-year-old man cry at the burning of his home so soon to be cleared of debt can doubt the relationship of some property to personality.

A second context in which property is related to persons would include any buildings in which people live or work or are otherwise present from time to time. A bomb set in a building to go off at night may be intended to avoid killing hundreds of workers, yet may kill or maim a night watchman or employees working overtime for personal or business reasons. One of the chief dangers about the sanctioning of damage or destruction of buildings is that sooner or later persons are killed or injured in the process.

A third question raised by the idea that "some property has no right to exist" is who makes the decision. Igal Roodenko of the War Resisters League in opposing such destruction wrote: "If I can say that some property does not deserve to exist I must permit everyone else to say the same."[15] This is what has been happening. On the night of May 9, 1969, the office of the War Resisters League in New York City was wrecked, addressing and mimeograph machines smashed, and the membership file and all mailing stencils were stolen. In the early morning of March 23, 1969 the building of the Women's International League for Peace and Freedom which also housed other peace groups was destroyed by a fire that seemed clearly the work of an arsonist.

15. Igal Roodenko, "The Draft Board Raids Debate," *WRL News*, November–December 1969.

Those who advocate the destruction of draft board files or the records of a firm making napalm for Vietnam indicate that "property must not be used in the service of death."[16] Alfred Hassler's response to this is that those who destroy property "to achieve their ends . . . release the System from its own conscientious misgivings, recruit supporters for it from among millions of the uneasy, noncommitted, and ignite the unstable Rightist Fringe into much less discriminating acts of violence of their own."[17] There may be some qualifications of that statement in the case of some property of a highly unpopular system. The destruction of draft files, for example, did not create any public outcry. But if we acknowledge that property has instrumental, rather than intrinsic, value, as in the case of persons, then we cannot take an absolutist position with respect to it. Instead, property that is not an extension of personality must be viewed strategically. For example, a rat-infested slum dwelling condemned by the city and no longer occupied could be destroyed after ascertaining that there were no chance visitors, such as children, playing in it and no risk to adjacent buildings if it were burned. One such burning might not pose any serious strategic problem. But if sixty thousand or even a thousand condemned dwellings in any city were systematically or simultaneously burned, the entire machinery of law and order would be mobilized, aggravating the fear and paranoia which is always to some degree present, thus providing the justification for increased repression.

The destruction of property in the United States must be viewed in the context of American values. The United States, which includes ordinary citizens as well as law-enforcement personnel, has viewed property as of more value than human life. This is the basic reason that neither police nor property owners are prosecuted when they shoot either

16. Jerry Elmer, "The Draft Board Raids Debate," *WRL News*, November–December 1969.

17. *Fellowship*, May 1970, p. 4.

adults or children in the act of stealing. Attorney General
Ramsey Clark was a voice crying in the wilderness when
he deplored the shooting of looters during riots as "sum-
mary capital punishment without trial" and a substitution
of bullets for trained policemen who could protect property
or make arrests without killing.[18]

It is possible that the destruction of draft board files will
help to deemphasize property values by asserting the priority of human life which the draft is instrumental in de-
meaning or destroying. But this must be judged in the light
of later developments, including the escalation of property
destruction. The pouring of blood on draft files in Baltimore in October 1967 aroused little public opposition. It
was followed in 1968 by the burning of draft file records in
Catonsville, Maryland. In both cases there was dramatic
public exposure and disruption without violence to anyone.
There was more controversy over the Catonsville incident
because of the statement used to justify it: "Some property
has no right to exist." The subsequent destruction of
ROTC buildings contributed little if anything to the exposure or disruption of the system. Instead such action became the occasion for greater government repression such
as the Kent State massacre of students.

On the other hand if property is not an absolute value,
certain judgments can be made about it. One is that it is
better to choose human values over property values. It is
also necessary to recognize that property whose sole purpose is to degrade or destroy human beings has disvalue
rather than value. Some who would agree to its disvalue
would argue for action that would force the government to
destroy or abandon such property whereas others would
respond that revolutionary action is not directed toward
governmental reform but uses the destruction of such
property to expose the nature of the government.

Every tactic in the final analysis must be judged by its

18. *New York Times*, 16 August 1968.

contribution to the overall strategy of the movement. Has it attracted more support to those engaged in the work of liberation? Has it influenced those in the middle who are neither staunch opponents nor supporters of liberation? Has it kept things moving so that hidden tensions are brought out into the open; so that conflict forces people to face the real issues? Tactics which never threaten the power structures of society or the privileges of the power elite can easily be dismissed. Martin Luther King, Jr. in his "Letter from Birmingham Jail" criticized "the white moderate who is more devoted to 'order' than to justice; who prefers a negative peace which is the absence of tension to a positive peace which is the presence of justice." Militants are more useful than moderates in inducing social change.

It is, however, essential to question any tactic which is elitist in nature, in which masses of people cannot participate and which goes to the brink of public misunderstanding. There is no virtue in actions which alienate substantial groups of people or which isolate people from the revolution. The important task is to create a new society and that means winning the people. The point in revolution is not one of seeking an outlet for one's rage; it is to build the widest possible support for new structures and for a new respect for persons. That support and the new structures necessarily involve strategies and tactics that expose, resist, and bypass the old oppressive structures.

10

STRATEGIES OF LIBERATION

IT IS NOT ENOUGH to criticize the covert violence in the existing structures or the overt violence of armed revolutions. The important question is how to think of liberating action. This requires either a model for revolution, or at least a strategy for moving in the direction of liberation.

The prerequisite for any revolutionary struggle is a community of the oppressed. Such a community could be a racial minority as evident in the case of black people in the United States or a racial majority such as black Africans in the Republic of South Africa. It could be rural or urban workers or the unemployed. It could also be an entire class such as those in lower economic levels. The community is not created by a group of intellectuals who believe in liberation but exists as a people who desperately need to be set free and have developed a sense of identity out of a common experience of oppression. Intellectuals may participate in the developing of their awareness of oppression or the planning of action but it is the community that shapes the values of those who take the lead for change.

The mere existence of a community of the oppressed

does not in itself mean that there is a revolutionary consciousness. Most and perhaps all oppressed groups have a limited understanding of the system that holds them down. They probably accept the system while simply wanting some change within it. The first task is therefore one of delegitimatizing the system, of publicly exposing its connection with oppression. Such public exposure also builds allies outside 'of the immediate community among those who dislike injustice or exploitation. This idea of exposure of systems was used dramatically in Alabama to unmask the pretensions and undermine the legitimacy of the racial caste system. White southerners had insisted for years that Negroes preferred to live in segregated communities, to use separate schools, lavatories, restaurants, and ride in the back of buses. Individual Negroes risked their jobs or homes or lives if they told their white employers or neighbors or other whites how they really felt about such white racism. To take such a stance would have marked them as radicals or agitators who were causing trouble. But the Montgomery, Alabama, bus boycott in which thousands of Montgomery blacks participated told the entire nation that black people did not prefer segregation and were prepared to suffer to prove it. Thousands walked long distances to work and other thousands traveled in crowded car pools. The same idea of unmasking the system, of "telling it like it is" occurred when millions of television viewers saw the brutality of Bull Connor's Birmingham, Alabama police, police dogs, and fire hoses directed at marching black women and children. Martin Luther King described the power of exposure in these words about the South: "Merely to march in public streets was to rock the *status quo* to its roots. : . . If they let us march, they admitted their lie that the black man was content. If they shot us down they told the world they were inhuman brutes."[1]

1. Martin Luther King, Jr., *The Trumpet of Conscience* (New York: Harper and Row, 1967), p. 5.

These demonstrations involved a collective statement both to the entire black minority in the United States as well as to the whites of the nation. Prior to such collective exposure of racism, Negroes said "yes" to the white master when they meant "no." To say one thing to the white man and the opposite to their own families was a disintegrating experience. To learn to tell the white man exactly what they felt, or in other words to speak the truth, was a liberating experience. By the process of speaking the truth to those in power they began also to believe in themselves and in their own ability to influence the course of events.

Similar exposure of the system occurred during the war in Vietnam when thousands of young men went to Canada to avoid the draft or refused induction or burned draft cards or turned them in at public ceremonies. For example: Immediately following the extension of the war into Cambodia and the killing of four Kent State University students by the National Guard, a draft resistance organization was formed at Princeton University called the Union for National Draft Opposition (UNDO). Chapters sprang up all over the country. At the first national conference, May 19–21, 1970, "there were about 110 known UNDO chapters and some twelve thousand draft cards were said to have been collected around the country."[2] Fourteen hundred draft cards and induction notices were publicly burned in Lares, Puerto Rico on September 30, 1970 in a demonstration attended by twenty thousand people.[3] Earlier, on October 27, 1967, a group led by the Reverend Philip H. Berrigan poured blood into the files of a Baltimore draft board office. On May 17, 1968 Berrigan and his brother, Reverend Daniel Berrigan, and seven other Catholic Christians burned with napalm six hundred individual draft files taken from a draft board office at Catonsville, Maryland. Their arrest while at prayer and their trial and

2. *Resist*, 30 May 1970.
3. *Resist*, 6 November 1970.

conviction increased the exposure of the draft. Conscription ceased to be simply a means of national defense and became evident as a system of exploitation. Conscription was inevitably linked with the war in Vietnam which itself was exposed by mass demonstrations, by TV and other films, by university "teach-ins," boycotts of war industry, stockholder confrontations, and numerous other tactics.

The process of exposure or unmasking of one or more systems is intended not only to open the eyes of large numbers of people but also to radicalize those who engage in such action. The radicalizing process is a result of attempts by the administrators of the system to discredit, impede, harass, arrest or otherwise do violence to those who oppose the system. The reason those who administer the systems try to stop the opponents of the system is their knowledge that all structures, governments, and systems require mass support to exist. The first step prior to a withdrawal of support or consent is for people to become aware that the system is in fact harmful rather than beneficial to them or other human beings.

This process of unmasking or exposing is imbedded in various traditions. Marxists speak of exposing the contradictions in a given system; they educate and agitate so as to win people away from capitalism or non-Communist imperialism. During the period of the New Left in the United States when college students by and large rejected Communist, Trotskyist or other forms of the Old Left, students experimented with methods of changing social structures. The *New Left Notes* of January 22, 1968, said, "One effective means of disruption is the tactic of exposure. For to delegitimatize the public relations image of an institution or person is to undermine its or his most sophisticated technique of control . . . the concealment of its or his real motivations."

There is a similar motif of public exposure in Christian thought. The apostle Paul said of Jesus that "He disarmed the principalities and powers and made a public example of

them, triumphing over them thereby."[4] By this he may
have meant that Jesus' continuing concern for his enemies
in contrast to the brutality of the crucifixion exposed the
dehumanizing efforts of the powers. In any event it is also
possible to say that Jesus made a public example of the
inflexibility of the Sabbath law when he openly broke it to
feed hungry people or to heal those who were sick. He was
also involved in unmasking a practice of exploiting people
when he drove the money changers from the temple. Martin Luther King, following the same approach, made a
public example of white racism by engaging in civil disobedience to discriminatory laws.

The idea of public exposure, of unmasking the powers or
systems, signals their ultimate defeat because they can no
longer function under cover of an implied goodness or
usefulness but must be seen in their true nature as enemies.
When they are seen as obvious enemies they arouse resistance.

Gandhi also linked the resistance to British imperialism
by the people of India to the idea of speaking the truth.
The Indian word *Satyagraha* that Gandhi used to describe
the nonviolent resistance to British rule of India literally
means "holding fast to truth" or truth force or soul force.
God is truth, according to Gandhi's belief, and he sought
truth through action. His method of action involved exposure of oppression through the public suffering of those
who resisted foreign rule. The public suffering was a direct
consequence of Indian noncooperation with British orders
or of civil disobedience to some particularly objectionable
system or tax.

An examination of the differences in approach to the
exposure of oppression reveals that the Marxist-Leninist
sees it chiefly as an aspect of agitation or a stage in the
development of a revolutionary situation which leads to a
predetermined method of violent revolution followed by

4. Col. 2:15.

dictatorship or rule from the top. Gandhians, on the other hand do not view the exposure of oppression as separate from or prior to their other actions of noncooperation, public suffering, etc. Their method is their goal for they see the continuing necessity of measuring every system by the search for truth. There is no postrevolutionary situation or rule from the top which precludes a continuing necessity of exposing systems. In this respect their approach is akin to the idea held by some Christians that there is a permanent necessity of revolution because every social structure falls short of the standards of God and must therefore be continually exposed and changed.

A second step in the direction of liberation is the organization of those who are oppressed. The approach to organizations will vary depending upon the group to be organized. Whatever the group, it is essential that decisions not be made at the top by one or a few leaders. Since one of the major purposes of liberation is to give power to the whole people, organizations must be structured so that the members make the decisions and thereby gain experience in decision making. Otherwise the arrest, exile or assassination of leaders may destroy the movement. Leaders also become ineffective if their followers lose interest from lack of participation in the making of decisions. But the deeper purpose is to move toward a decentralized control of the structure of society by the method of decentralized democratic decision making. The end is determined by the means.

It is possible that an effective organization will grow out of loosely organized action campaigns, but any people concerned with liberation must begin to experiment with methods for achieving their purpose. This experimentation could begin with role playing, wherein people simulate a conflict situation and try various methods of dealing with it. In addition there is a value in vigiling, marching, picketing, or other concrete action with others against a specific injustice. These help build group solidarity and courage as well as experience. Such experiments should fit within the overall strategy of gaining power for the whole people as suggested below.

One of the major strategies of liberation is that of non-cooperation with a specific system or government. This is based on the fact that all systems and governments thrive by cooperation and actually exist only with the consent of the people. It is more difficult to refuse cooperation with a totalitarian or otherwise repressive government than with a relatively democratic one. Noncooperation, however, is more possible and more effective than many other methods under such circumstances. In 1954, a group of Negroes in Orangeburg, South Carolina, petitioned for integrated schools. The white community retaliated by stopping milk and bread deliveries to the homes of those signing the petition, by foreclosing mortgages, and other similar action. From that point on no black student in either of the two Negro colleges in Orangeburg would buy or drink milk, eat bread, or purchase Coca-Cola. The power of a boycott lies in the fact that no one can compel a person to buy and use a certain product. Such a refusal to cooperate in the purchasing or using of a product can be undertaken even in police states.

An unintended by-product of the Montgomery, Alabama, bus boycott was the incidental boycott of white business and shops in the center city. Black people who walked or had to travel in car pools could neither take the time to shop "downtown" nor carry packages home. The unintended boycott encouraged the affected white businessmen to become allies of the blacks in seeking an early and favorable settlement of the bus boycott.

The boycott, which is most effective when a government's or corporation's financial success depends on a certain volume of business, is not the only form of noncooperation. Other forms are draft resistance, student strikes, labor strikes, boycott of elections, sit-ins, picketing, civil disobedience, and various forms of disruption.

The United Farm Workers Organizing Committee (UFWOC) and its leader, Cesar Chavez, combined a strike, a boycott, and some of the tactics of the civil rights movement such as mobilizing students and churchmen to march, picket, and collect food and money for the strikers. The strike began in 1965 with a group of AFL-CIO Filipino grape thinners. Chavez and the Mexican-American farm workers who joined the strike knew that it would be broken unless it had outside help. They got help first from the California Migrant Ministry, a Protestant group, and then from civil rights groups such as the Congress of Racial Equality and the Student Nonviolent Coordinating Committee. The ministers and civil rights workers helped organize and man the picket lines for thirty large ranches which covered roughly 400 square miles. The pickets were bound to a strategy of nonviolence but on some occasions did not stick to it. "Growers walked up and down the picket line, stamping on the toes of the strikers, tripping them up . . ." They also "drove down the edge of their property with spraying machines, shooting insecticide and fertilizer on the pickets, or gunned over the roadside in tractors raising dust to choke the strikers."[5]

Chavez and his colleagues retaliated by testifying at government hearings on pesticides. Harry Bridge's longshoremen refused to load the grapes from the San Francisco docks to outward-bound vessels. Then, California Catholic bishops publicly supported the right of farm workers to organize. Such support was not enough and Chavez called for a nation-wide boycott. The boycott was focused first on Schenley Industries, Inc., because liquor was easy to boycott. The AFL-CIO unions across the country joined the boycott. A staff of people under twenty-five years of age went to thirteen major cities across the nation after having left Delano, California, penniless. They "hitchhiked or rode the rails," begged housing, food, an office, and

5. John Gregory Dunne, "Strike!" *Saturday Evening Post*, 6 May 1967, p. 38.

telephone. They "recruited some 10,000 people to pass out leaflets or to telephone neighbors, friends, churches and stores, urging support of the boycott."[6] Schenley was the first to sign a contract with Chavez.

The boycott spread to fifty-three major grape-consuming cities, and by September 1970, seventy percent of California's grape growers had signed contracts with UFWOC. The boycott succeeded in reducing sales by thirty percent. It also "forced thousands of tons of grapes into cold storage and confronted growers with the bleak prospect of economic disaster if they persisted" in the exploitation of the workers.[7] One of the important factors in the victory was the fear held by large corporations, who were also involved in the grape industry, of the damage to their "corporate image built up over many years with the expenditure of millions of dollars in advertising and public relations contracts."[8]

Another type of noncooperation, civil disobedience, is a political act designed to focus attention either upon an unjust law or a government in order to change it. It is therefore a deliberate and public refusal to obey. In a nation with a democratic tradition rational disobedience to a specific law is not considered a revolutionary act but may be the only means to test the validity of that law or to obey conscience. Civil disobedience is nevertheless revolutionary when masses of people defy a government or a system sanctioned by the government as the Gandhians did in refusing to obey British laws. It may even be revolutionary if small groups of people disobey laws that are not customarily disobeyed by men of conscience. For example, conscientious objectors in the United States have traditionally refused military inductions when government draft boards break the law by denying deferments to such objec-

6. Ibid., p. 50.
7. Victor Salandini, "Lessons of the Grape Strike," *America*, 17 October 1970, p. 285.
8. Ibid., p. 286.

tors. But the destruction of draft files in May 1968 by the group known as the Catonsville Nine and their use of the slogan, "Some property has no right to exist," was in the revolutionary tradition of the Boston Tea Party. Their act sparked a continuing succession of similar acts. By April 1970, more than a million draft files in over 150 boards throughout the country had been destroyed.[9] Although the Catonsville Nine and some other groups that followed their example disobeyed the law, their act was more in the nature of disruption than the mere refusal to obey the requirements of law which is characteristic of civil disobedience.

Disruption goes beyond the act of noncooperation or even disobedience to dramatize an unjust law; it involves an effort to stop the functioning of a law, a system or an institution. Disruption of a meeting can take place without a word or without much activity. A hundred persons in the front of a meeting to support or rationalize war, for example, need only place death masks over their faces, rise in their places, and remain standing. Martin Luther King shortly before his death talked of mass civil disobedience as necessary in the North. He came to the conclusion that the marches and demonstrations adequate for the South were not effective in the North, so he said, "There must be more than a statement to the larger society; there must be a force that interrupts its functioning at some key point." He wanted to take the "deep rage of the ghetto manifest in riots and channel it into a constructive and creative force. To dislocate the functioning of a city without destroying it can be more effective than a riot because it can be longer lasting, costly to the larger society, but not wantonly destructive."[10]

There have not been many instances of disruption in the United States. But the Mayday actions in Washington, D.C., in 1971, involving more than fifteen thousand people

9. *Resist*, 24 April 1970.
10. Martin Luther King, Jr., *Conscience*, p. 15.

who were intent on disrupting traffic and government work is a significant illustration of what disruption could be. Prior to the planned disruption several hundred thousand people went to Washington to demonstrate against the war in Vietnam. Thousands stayed to engage in sit-ins or passive civil disobedience at government offices. Nicholas von Hoffman wrote in the *Washington Post* about the thousands of disrupters who had "turned this capital city into a simulated Saigon with the choppers flying all over, the armed men everywhere, and the fear that at any moment something worse . . . might happen."[11]

Noam Chomsky suggests that "the Pentagon demonstrations of 1967, with the threat of further disruption, were a factor in leading to a change of strategy after the Tet offensive. The belief that the country would be torn apart by overt escalation was surely a factor in the decision not to send an additional 200,000 troops to Vietnam, and to readjust the bombing in Indochina."[12]

All noncooperation on a large scale involves public exposure of the system and also coercion of those who are in any way involved in supporting or profiting from the system. It assumes that there is power in withdrawing support from oppressive or exploiting structures. There is also a moral power that comes from saying "No" to a monstrous evil that formerly one supported simply because it was the law or accepted custom or economic practice. Refusal to cooperate is a weapon that the apparently weak or less powerful or the "underdog" can use. It does not require physical strength or economic wealth. It requires other elements of strength such as determination and a willingness to sacrifice. Gandhi points out in his "Doctrine of the Sword" that "strength does not come from physical capacity. It comes from an indomitable will."

11. Washington Post, 5 May 1971.
12. Noam Chomsky, "Mayday: The Case for Civil Disobedience," *The New York Review of Books*, 17 June 1971, p. 26.

Another major strategy of liberation is the usurpation of some function of a system or the taking possession of some property in order to decrease the powerlessness of the oppressed. The "sit-in" used by black students in restaurants and other places in the South in the 1950s and 1960s is a moderate form of usurpation.

In 1964 the Bank of America agreed to hire eight thousand Negroes and Mexican-Americans as the result of a hundred-day-long action campaign by twenty-six California chapters of the Congress of Racial Equality (CORE). In many cities CORE picketed and held sit-ins in the banks. They also engaged in "coin-ins," a device for stalling business by lining up at tellers' windows to get change. As a result of the action other smaller banks "voluntarily" decided to hire blacks in small numbers.[13]

A more revolutionary illustration of usurpation was the land invasion in Peru under the leadership of Hugo Blanco. Beginning in 1958, Blanco organized about one hundred fifty rural syndicates or unions in the valley of La Convención. These unions organized strikes of *colonos* or Indian peasants who worked a plot of land on a *hacienda*. The *colonos* refused to perform any service for the *hacienda* but continued to cultivate the plots of land that had been designated for their own use. The landowners had to pay wages to their peasants or go out of business. Later the unions started invading the *haciendas*. The *colonos* claimed the ownership of the land they had been tilling as feudal tenants. They also took control of unused land and divided it among the landless Indians. "Some of the peasants were armed, but there was very little shooting and no burning and looting of *haciendas*. . . . In most cases the owner was left in possession of that part of the *hacienda* which had always been worked for his account. But if he wanted labor to work this land he would now have to pay for it."[14]

13. *CORE-LATOR*, September–October, 1964.
14. Robert Marett, *Peru* (New York: Praeger, 1969), pp. 222, 223.

The peasants were revolutionary in their invasion of *haciendas* not only because they were not interested in improving their position within the traditional master-serf system but also because they formed unions and organized their own communities independently of the government. These unions "secured total control in numerous regions, especially the valleys of La Convención and de Lares in the Department of Cuzco where nuclei of autonomous power based on the peasantry now exists."[15] In some places such as Colombia, Venezuela, and Guatemala there were armed invasions by guerrillas who intended to seize the land for the peasants, but in Peru with some exceptions the armed elitist approach was rejected; "the emphasis . . . was on mass mobilization, large scale participation around immediate demands—'those who till the land shall own it' and the use of relatively non-violent direct action . . ."[16]

Andre Gorz reports a usurpation case in Italy. There was a large

mechanical construction enterprise at Reggio Emilia condemned to be shut down as part of the Marshall Plan, whose entire personnel (workers and staff) occupied the plant, threw out the management, and making use of abandoned projects, organized the production of agricultural tractors on its own initiative. It took several months before the first tractors came off the assembly lines. During this entire time, the company was able to keep going thanks to the funds raised among the peasant and urban population of the region. A rough hewn Commune, this venture was finally refinanced by the State, under the pressure of the working class parties.[17]

In the United States there have been usurpations or seizures of property for temporary purposes. The sit-down

15. James Petras and Maurice Zeitlin, eds., *Latin America: Reform or Revolution* (Greenwich, Conn.: Fawcett Publications, 1968), p. 343.

16. Ibid., p. 344.

17. Andre Gorz, *Strategy for Labor* (Boston: Beacon Press, 1971), p. 59.

strikes by workers in the automobile plants in Detroit in 1937, and the sit-ins by black students in restaurants or other places of public accommodation in the 1950s, were temporary invasions of property as over against permanent seizures. A similar approach was followed in the Freedom Rides when black and white people integrated buses traveling through southern states. In New York City in 1970, there was an occupation of Lincoln Hospital in the Puerto Rican community by a coalition of groups which included the Young Lords Party, the Health Revolutionary Unity movement, which unites black and Puerto Rican hospital workers, and some New Left doctors at the hospital. Their purpose was to get the hospital to serve the needs of the community instead of continuing as an elitist institution. An incident of hospital neglect that resulted in the death of a Puerto Rican child led to an invasion of the hospital by crowds who refused to leave without some steps being taken toward community control. Their "demands included the setting up of grievance committees and a complaint table in the hospital, with community participation." They also asked for "street clinics and door-to-door preventive medical measures."

When they occupied the hospital they set up barricades but they did not engage in any shoot-out or fight with the police when the police eventually decided to attack. David Dellinger described the situation as follows:

To have had guns and to have used them would have confused the issues and interfered with continued community and public support. Force, yes—the occupation of the building, the erection of barricades, a subsequent take-over of a portable x-ray unit to take it to the streets where the people were. But self in-dulgent trashing of the hospital or offing of pigs, no. So strong was the community support, that all charges against the invaders were dropped.[18]

18. David Dellinger, "A Time to Look at Ourselves," *Liberation,* Autumn 1970, p. 13.

The invasion did not accomplish "instant revolution" but it did bring the community together to control "one area of its life" and it brought "other young doctors who think that medicine exists to serve the people" to the Lincoln staff.[19]

The idea of usurpation was tried by Indians under Gandhi's leadership as early as 1930 when they fought the British salt monopoly by making salt from ocean water contrary to the orders of the colonial government. Usurpation, however, has not been widely used by any group of people and needs much more experimentation. It would probably have its greatest potential in large landed estates where *campesinos* or peasants are already living and working on the land but decide to sell their own crops cooperatively and refuse to pay rent to absentee landlords; or in a factory which workers occupy for the purpose of continued production under the direction of a workers' council which they elect. In such cases the government is likely to try to drive the peasants or workers off the property or force them to return to old ways. It is obviously essential that any efforts to stop usurpation be met nonviolently and with maximum publicity through unofficial channels if the usual media such as newspapers, TV, and radio do not report the government action.

Each campaign requires its own appropriate methods of communication. This is especially true of strategies of usurpation which are carved out in isolated areas. The purpose of usurpation is to alter the structures of ownership and/or control so that the community involved in the action may either control or participate in the control. The intention is to get the government or its enforcing arm to accept the new system of the nonviolent usurpers.

A fourth strategy of liberation is the formation of parallel or alternate systems or governments. By a parallel system or government we mean a structure that the revolutionary movement establishes to take over the necessary functions of the system or government that is to be re-

19. Ibid.

placed. A parallel government or system is in reality an extension of the strategy of usurpation because some or all of the functions of government are usurped when a parallel structure is set up. The classic illustration is the Congress party in India to which the followers of Gandhi gave their allegiance instead of to the British government. The parallel government was thus already in existence and functioning when the British agreed to India's independence. A nonrevolutionary illustration of a parallel system is the cooperative movement which at one time thought of itself as an alternative to capitalism which would grow in the midst of capitalism and eventually replace it. Any revolutionary group that wanted to resist capitalism, as some black militants have talked of doing, could create their own cooperatives to reinforce the rest of their struggle.

Not every system that is to be eliminated requires that a parallel structure be set up by those engaged in resisting the system. Those who oppose conscription, for example, may also oppose the entire military system and hence not be willing to encourage any alternative to conscription.

The currently popular word *counterculture* is viewed by some as an unplanned parallel society whose values will replace those of the existing American culture. Some would go so far as to say that this has already happened in the way long hair, unorthodox dress, and other counterculture values have already invaded business and other circles than the hippie and student milieu where such styles are thought to have originated. Others argue that the freedom to dress and wear hair differently, to use drugs, or in other ways demonstrate a counterculture is not very revolutionary since no significant political or economic changes are implicit in it, as evident by the appropriation of such styles by many in business and political circles. Jacques Ellul has a different analysis of counterculture which suggests that it is not really an alternative structure. He writes:

In a way I admire the hippie movement but I do not believe that such a movement can result in any worthwhile development of action. The hippies, whether they like it or not, are merely a luxury phenomenon in a "great society." The technological society and the power it commands form the infrastructure without which the hippies could not exist. The radicalism I am in search of is much more basic. . . . it is only through complete refusal to compromise with the forms and forces of our society that we can find the right orientation and recover the hope of human freedom.[20]

Much of the counterculture thinking fails to come to grips with Ellul's criticism and therefore has limited value in terms of social change.

At least one counterculture movement has been related to political social change. This is the commune or collective envisioned as a group in revolt against bourgeois morals and politics. One such commune in Berkeley which subscribed to a document called "Revolutionary Families" spent a great deal of time on sexual liberation, including discussing "smashing monogamy." One member of the commune reported:

Smashing monogamy, at least the way we were talking about it, was a male trip . . . in retrospect it had also been the men who had always talked the most about sexual liberation and who had initiated what ill-fated sexual experimentation had actually taken place. It is tempting to attribute this solely to the men's desire to sleep with many women, and this undoubtedly played a part. But I think the explanation is far more insidious than the mere *physical* excitement and satisfaction gained from sexual variety. To be a successful movement male, one has to prove that as well as being intelligent, militant, and articulate, that he is also sexually liberated. . . . It was not even the desire for the women as sexual objects, much less as human beings, that primarily motivated the men. Rather it was the need to establish their image among the men, and their position in the social hierarchy of the house.[21]

20. Jacques Ellul, "Mirror of These Ten Years," *The Christian Century*, 18 February 1970, p. 203.
21. "Wish I Could Give All I Wanted to Give: Thoughts on

Communes are intended either to bypass the traditional monogamous family or in some cases to be a collective of families. There is an assumption that the traditional nuclear family is either no longer viable or represents a "bourgeois propertied relationship" in which one person tries to possess another. It is too simplistic to suggest that the commune will not face the same problems that are sometimes destructive of traditional family life. "Like any other presently existing social unity, a commune," wrote a member of one in Berkeley, "is permeated with hierarchy, competition and domination. There are structural incentives which induce psychological violence. There are real things to be won and lost. The collective interest of revolutionaries is not much more harmonious than that of any other social group."[22] The trap in which many commune members apparently fall is that of believing that economic possessiveness or domination is an essential characteristic of a monogamous family and that a rearrangement of sleeping habits is a departure from bourgeois practice. The objection of the Left to bourgeois practices is that they are exploitative and dehumanizing. But any sexual activity can be basically exploitative. And bourgeois society has produced a variety of sexual activity, much of which is both dehumanizing and unrelated to monogamy. The linking of sexual freedom to counterculture movements can be analyzed as a protest against monogamy, but it can also be viewed as a more sophisticated extension of the existing male sexual culture. As such, the real counterculture is women's liberation, which is intended to take place within as well as outside the marriage relationship. Linda Phelps strikes this note in saying:

The so-called sexual revolution has turned sour. The end of inhibition and the release of sexual energies which have so often

---

Living in a Political Commune," *Liberation*, Autumn 1970, p. 27.
    22. Ibid., p. 30.

been documented as the innovation of the revolutionary culture are now beginning to be seen as just another fraud. . . . Sexual freedom has meant more opportunity for men, not a new kind of experience for women.[23]

Sexual liberation is not a rationale for male aggression or promiscuity or an unending variety of sexual experiences, but a mutual expression of caring, trust, pleasure, and support. These are usually the product of a faithful rather than casual relationship. Sexual liberation is also the change in relationship from a male-dominated society to one where men and women are genuinely equal. In this respect the women's liberation movement is consciously political as well as counterculture. It is probably the most significant aspect of counterculture, far more important than gay liberation. Gay liberation can hope for acceptance of homosexuals and for society's respect and equal treatment; it cannot hope to replace heterosexuality; neither is it likely to change society as profoundly as the political, economic, and social equality of women will do.

Christopher Lasch in *The New York Review of Books* of October 21, 1971, rightly points to a deeper economic and political problem that underlies sexual mores:

the system that forces women (and men also) to choose between home and work is the same system that demands early specialization and prolonged schooling, imposes militarylike discipline in all areas of work, and forces not only factory workers but intellectual workers into a ruthless competition for meager rewards.

The solution to this problem is not to be found in a few rural communes. The urban technological society cannot be reversed by a back-to-the-land movement. Neither is the urban commune under existing conditions likely to be

23. Linda Phelps, "Death in the Spectacle: Female Sexual Alienation," *Liberation*, May 1971, p. 23.

much more than a dormitory from which members go out to work within the same system.

What is genuine counterculture and what is simply an extension of the existing dehumanizing culture is open to analysis and dispute. For the purpose of discussing revolutionary strategy it is sufficient to say that the creation of a new way of life would be as revolutionary as the creation of a new system parallel to the old. What is necessary is that masses of people choose to cooperate with the new and to reject and resist the old.

Any creation of a new center of loyalty interferes with and to some degree restricts or nullifies the power of the former center of loyalty. This was evident in the creation of Protestant churches during the Reformation, which in some countries led to the virtual disappearance of Roman Catholic influence. It was evident during the Nazi period in some countries in Western Europe such as Norway and Denmark, where citizens engaged in nonviolent resistance to imposed regimes by accepting resistance movements as their new center of loyalty.

The creation of a parallel system or government is intended to establish a new center of loyalty or new way of life which in itself is a form of noncooperation with the existing oppressive system. It is therefore intended as a device to aid in the collapse of the old. It also serves as a vehicle of transition into a new order and can become the administrative mechanism of the new society.

The combination of exposure of oppressive systems, the organization of the oppressed, their noncooperation with one or more systems, their usurpation of land or factories or services and the creation of parallel structures would create far-reaching changes in any society. These, however, are not the only strategies that might be effective in achieving liberation from existing systems. The human imagination is capable of producing many different approaches to systemic change.

It is possible that students could force a reorganization

of the ideology and structure of the universities so that they ceased to be controlled by existing corporate and political systems for their benefit. The preparation for living in a new society would to some degree eventuate in new systems and values.

It is possible, for example, where a revolutionary situation exists, to plan a confrontation with the government by means of a general strike. Such a plan would depend on a revolutionary labor movement or a spontaneous uprising of the people. There have been such popular uprisings in Latin America other than the Guatemalan incident described in chapter four.

In Chile, President Carlos Ibáñez del Campo, a military dictator, was overthrown in July 1931. He had ruled since the July 1927 coup d'état that had brought him to power. When he was ousted, Chile was in the midst of an economic depression with world prices being down on copper and nitrate, two of her chief products. Ibáñez had an extensive spy system and had deprived the people of their rights, imposing restrictions on free speech and on the press. During the economic crisis there were various resignations from his cabinet. When Pedro Blanquier, the second premier in a month, resigned, there were demonstrations. Students at the National University and the Catholic University voted a four-day strike "in commemoration of the four days of liberty" that Premier Blanquier had provided in granting freedom of the press, postponing conscription calls, and permitting exiles to return to Chile.

On July 22, students took control of the main university building, hanging out a banner with the word LIBERTAD in large letters. Others demonstrated in the streets. The next day an ultimatum was given to the students by the new premier, a Navy captain, Carlos Froedden, giving students until 10:00 P.M. to leave the university or risk coming under fire. The medical association voted to call a city-wide strike if any students were injured. The students retaliated by demanding Ibáñez's resignation. When the troops drove the students from the university on July 24 they killed two students.

The bar association decided to join the medical doctors in supporting the students. "A meeting of prominent citizens called by the President was unattended. Strikes of school teachers, engineers, clerks and other workers inaugurated a policy of passive resistance to the government and a general strike was considered." President Ibáñez was forced to turn over authority to the president of the senate. The military cabinet resigned and Ibáñez fled to Argentina. Amnesty for exiled and imprisoned political offenders was declared, the state police were confined to barracks and students directed traffic.[24]

There was a similar action taken in El Salvador in 1944 against the president, General Maximiliano Hernández Martínez, who had taken control of the country in 1931 by means of a military coup. He kept the army and public employees happy with high pay but was ruthless in liquidating his opponents. On April 2, 1944, an army officer, Colonel Tito Calvo, and his followers took control of part of the capital including two radio stations which announced that the government had been overthrown. Hernández Martínez fled to the national police headquarters and rallied forces for a counterattack. After retaking the city he executed Tito Calvo.[25]

An estimated three thousand Salvadorans had been killed and five thousand more were jailed by Martínez. Sixty-two truckloads of peasants who were headed for San Salvador to demonstrate were machine-gunned in an ambush. People were tortured in an effort to make them divulge the names of conspirators. The archbishop asked for an end to the slaughter but Hernández insultingly rejected his overture.

When a faculty member was condemned to death for

24. Henry Gratton Doyle, "Chilean Dictatorship Overthrown," *Current History* 34 (September 1931), p. 918.
25. *Newsweek*, 17 April 1944, p. 65.

participating in the revolt university students issued the following call:

Decree for a general strike including hospitals, courts and public works. . . . The basis of the strike shall be general passive resistance, non cooperation with the government, the wearing of mourning, the unity of all classes, the prohibition of fiestas.

By showing the tyrant the abyss between him and the people by isolating him completely, we shall cause his downfall. Boycott the movies, the newspapers, the national lottery. Pay no taxes. Abandon government jobs. Leave them unfilled. Pray daily for the souls of the massacred. The Archbishop has been humiliated.[26]

The university and public school students were the first to strike. By April 27, all cars and buses had stopped running. The next day federal and municipal employees walked out. Then the railway workers struck. Women dressed in mourning marched silently in the streets of El Salvador. On May 5, sixty of the medical staff at Rosales Hospital joined the strike and all doctors' offices closed. By May 6, stores, banks, factories, and commercial offices were closed. "There was no traffic, no transportation. Everyone but the police stayed at home." On May 8, Hernández met with the cabinet to discuss what to do. All but one of them suggested his resignation. The next day the national assembly accepted his resignation and Hernández took refuge in the Mexican embassy. But the people would not go back to work until he left the country.

The general strike ended after Hernández fled and after there was an unconditional amnesty granted by the new president to all political prisoners. One of the by-products was "freedom of the press for the first time in thirteen years."[27] In the case of El Salvador, Chile, and Guatemala (discussed in chapter four) the people demonstrated that

26. *Newsweek*, 22 May 1944, p. 66.
27. Ibid.

they could bring the government down by a combination of strikes, boycotts, and demonstrations. The power of noncooperation in each case was great enough to force a ruthless dictator to leave the country. But there was no revolution. The people insisted on certain freedom but within the same system. There was no organization of persons to take charge and point the way; there was no planning for anything different economically or politically; there was no long-term ferment among the people so that they saw other options or could desire them. The process of noncooperation was not aided by any strategy of parallel government so that a new structure could take over when the government collapsed. Instead people reverted to the familiar system except for demanding certain reforms.

Only in Guatemala did the change in government create the possibility of a continuing revolution. But the Arbenz administration, which followed the first democratically elected government after the dictator Ubico was ousted, was crushed by a CIA-sponsored invasion after the process of nationalization of land had begun. The United States action against Guatemala suggests another failure in planning for revolution. No effort had been made to build support in other countries either for the revolution or for the right to make basic economic changes. In the United States, for example, there had been no preparation of groups sympathetic to change in Latin America so they could have built a movement against United States intervention.

One difficulty in using illustrations of massive noncooperation with government as in Guatemala, El Salvador, and Chile is that such narratives perpetuate the idea that revolution is a sudden forcing of the collapse of a government. Instead revolution is a long-term process which may culminate in a dramatic seizure of power or may be consummated by a series of changes which can be described as the progressive conquest of power. The assumption that revolutions necessarily are accomplished in one great upheaval has been nourished by many socialists. However, a new type of socialist philosopher, Andre Gorz, suggests:

> If socialism is to result from the prolongation of the present day struggles and demands, it cannot be presented straight off as a whole system, as a solution which precedes all problems. It should be presented instead as a general direction in which concrete solutions to specific problems move.[28]

Gorz concludes, as does this author, that neither power nor nationalization are ends in themselves but must mean an end to exploitation, "a new type of relationship among men, a new order of priorities, a new model of life and of culture."[29] This suggests that the transformation of society will probably not take place later if there is not some transformation of personal and power relationships in the accomplishment of intermediate objectives. The virtue in the nonviolent strategies and illustrations used in this chapter is that they can be used to achieve intermediate objectives. It is of fundamental importance, however, that partial victories gained by such strategies not be absorbed by the system but be conceived as steps toward decentralization of decision-making power and therefore a restriction on both the political power of the state and the economic power of capital.

28. Gorz, *Strategy for Labor*, p. 12.
29. Ibid.

11

STEPS TOWARD BLACK LIBERATION

THE ROAD to black liberation began more than a century ago with the Emancipation Proclamation, but that was a technical end to legalized slavery. It did not mean freedom in the sense that Martin Luther King understood it when he said: "I have a dream that one day every Negro in this country, every colored person in the world, will be judged on the basis of the content of his character rather than the color of his skin, and every man will respect the dignity and worth of human personality." King included in his dream of liberation freedom from hunger, because genuine respect for personality implies, as he put it, that "the empty stomachs of Mississippi will be filled."

It is difficult to find a contemporary beginning point when it can be said that black people began to insist on being liberated. In one sense the turning point was the decision of a black family named Brown to challenge segregated education. Certainly the *Brown* v. *Topeka Board of Education* case in 1954 convinced many Negroes that the Supreme Court at least was prepared for changes to take place if black people would initiate them. But the roots of the first important struggles in which black people in any numbers participated can be traced to the nonviolent labor victories of the 1930s. In the conflict between General Motors and the CIO, General Motors refused to engage in collective bargaining, stockpiled their plants with gas and guns and hired an extensive labor spy apparatus. The black and white workers responded by engaging in a sit-down strike within the plants where General Motors's guns and gas could not be used without jeopardizing the property. The sit-downers, under very strict discipline, did not engage in property destruction and therefore did not provoke General Motors or the governor to drive the men out. The governor, Frank Murphy, took the position that if state police or troops were to be used it was to deal with violence and to maintain public order.[1]

In 1941, A. Philip Randolph, president of the Brotherhood of Sleeping Car Porters, with the assistance of black staff members of the Fellowship of Reconciliation, organized a "March on Washington." This march was to involve "a mass Negro convergence on Washington unless President Roosevelt secured employment for Negroes in the defense industries." The result was the "President's Executive Order 8802" which established a federal Fair Employment Practices Commission and thus "forestalled the demonstrations."[2] Many Negroes began to know what it was to have a regular job and a share in the wartime prosperity of the country. But even with money in their pockets there were many places they could not go. It seemed natural at that time to begin to open up restaurants, theaters, bowling alleys, and other places of public accommodation for everyone.

During the early years of World War II, A. J. Muste, James Farmer, Bayard Rustin, and other staff members of

1. Nat Hentoff, *The Essays of A. J. Muste* (Indianapolis: Bobbs Merrill, 1967), pp. 205–06.
2. *Report of the National Advisory Commission on Civil Disorders* (New York: Bantam Book, 1968), p. 223.

the Fellowship of Reconciliation (including this writer) decided to combine "Gandhi's techniques with the sit-in derived from the sit-down strikes of the 1930s." They did this through a series of training sessions in major northern and border cities, with the result that in a score of cities, such as Denver, Detroit, and Cleveland, local groups began campaigns to desegregate restaurants, stores, theaters, and other places of public accommodation. They also organized the Congress of Racial Equality (CORE) which was to continue the nonviolent attack on segregation.[3] George Houser was first Director of CORE. "In 1947 in conjunction with the Fellowship of Reconciliation, CORE conducted a 'Journey of Reconciliation'—that would later be called a 'Freedom Ride'—in the upper South, to begin the practice of desegregating buses in compliance with the recent Supreme Court decision outlawing segregation in interstate travel."[4]

The next step taken was a campaign to desegregate the armed forces. In 1947, the President's Committee on Civil Rights announced that Negroes "are faced by an absolute bar against enlistment in any branch of the Marine Corps other than the stewards' branch. . . ." The same report indicated that "almost 80 percent of the Negro sailors are serving as cooks, stewards, and steward's mates. . . . Less than one Negro in 70 in the Army is commissioned, while there is one white officer for every seven white enlisted men." This was an intolerable situation which Negro organizations wanted to end, but letters and visits to Congressmen did not result in desegregation. In the fall of 1947, Bayard Rustin, William Worthy, and this writer began discussions looking toward the formation of a Committee Against Discrimination in Military Service and Training which would use nonviolent direct action. The committee, which was formed in November 1947, soon changed its name to the Committee Against Jim Crow in

3. Ibid.
4. Ibid., p. 225.

Military Training and Service. The chairman of the committee, Grant Reynolds, a New York State commissioner, and the treasurer, A. Philip Randolph, who was president of the Brotherhood of Sleeping Car Porters, were able to secure the agreement of key Republicans, including Robert Taft, the majority leader in the Senate, and Joseph Martin, Speaker of the House, to support an amendment in any universal military training bill "barring all racial distinctions."

President Truman, who feared rising Negro concern as well as these Republican commitments, ordered Secretary of Defense Forrestal in February 1948, to end racial and religious segregation in the armed forces. Within a week Secretary of the Army Kenneth Royall, who had discussed the problem with the most influential southern members of the House and Senate Armed Services Committees, stated he was convinced that segregation of Negroes was "in the interest of national defense and both the staff and I feel that this is still the case." Shortly thereafter A. Philip Randolph told the Senate Armed Services Committee in a public hearing that he would ask Negroes all over the country to engage in a "civil disobedience protest" and "recommend that Negroes take no part in the Army." Grant Reynolds, a former army officer, also told the committee: "I personally will not re-enter a Jim Crow army if the age categories should include me."

A poll of 2,200 black college students on twenty-six campuses showed seventy-one percent in favor of such civil disobedience. Nevertheless Senator Richard Russell in May 1948, tried to maintain racial segregation by amending a bill for universal military training. His amendment was lost in committee by a seven to four vote. Thereafter the bill to adopt universal military training was shelved because southern Senators would not accept a desegregated army, and Republican leaders would not permit a bill to pass without an amendment against continued segregation. The *New York Times* of May 12, 1948, indicated that the original cause of the problem—Senator Russell's amend-ment—"was the recent starting of a 'civil disobedience movement' against the draft—a pledged refusal by either Negroes or whites to serve in a 'Jim Crow army' even under a selective draft system."

It was this threat of a civil disobedience movement plus the Congressional response to it that led to the policy of desegregation which the armed forces adopted in 1949.

But it was not until the Montgomery, Alabama bus boy-cott "captured the imagination of the nation and the Negro community in particular" that the present mood of black liberation began to develop on a nationwide basis. Martin Luther King at the beginning of the boycott had armed guards around his house and an armed bodyguard preced-ing and following his car wherever he went. Bayard Rustin and Glenn Smiley of the Fellowship of Reconciliation, who went to Montgomery shortly after the boycott began, were influential in persuading Dr. King to adopt a completely nonviolent policy. There were others among the black min-isters of Montgomery who had already had some experi-ence with nonviolent action because of their participation in the northern sit-ins during World War II.

The drama of the Montgomery boycott and its success led to similar movements in Tallahassee and other cities. In 1956, the Fellowship of Reconciliation called a Southwide strategy conference at which Martin Luther King, Ralph Abernathy, and two militant black leaders from each deep southern state were present. At that meeting the idea of a Southwide, nonviolent strategy and network was discussed, which in 1957 became the foundation for the Southern Christian Leadership Conference. (Among the whites pres-ent were A. J. Muste, Glenn Smiley, Will Campbell, and this writer.)

The Montgomery bus boycott was won by a combina-tion of factors. Prior to that boycott southern Negroes had covered up their real feelings so long that many whites believed Negroes preferred, or at least did not object to, a segregated status. The massive participation of the black community was the beginning of group "truth-telling" to the white community. The group said what many individuals were not yet prepared to tell their white employers, that they were no longer going to accept segregation without active resistance. The Montgomery success was a necessary first step in convincing black men that they were as good as any white men and could stand up to any white opposition the South might muster. The second factor in the success of the boycott was the pressure of the white merchants in the center city. Their businesses suffered when black people stopped buying from their stores solely because they were walking or riding in crowded cars and hence could not buy "downtown." This unintended boycott of center-city merchants led these businessmen to bring pressure on the city and the bus company for a settlement. The third factor was the court decision obtained by NAACP lawyers in November 1956, requiring desegregation of the buses. "In 1957 . . . Tuskegee Negroes undertook a three-year boycott of local merchants after the state legislature gerrymandered nearly all of the Negro voters outside of the town boundaries." The boycott set the stage for an NAACP lawsuit which led the Supreme Court to declare the "Tuskegee gerrymander illegal."[5]

In April 1960 Martin Luther King called together a group of students at Raleigh, North Carolina, to form the Student Nonviolent Coordinating Committee (SNCC). SNCC in 1961 with cooperation from CORE and the NAACP began voter registration campaigns in the counties and cities of Mississippi. Although there was little success at first, the Mississippi Freedom Democratic party started by SNCC made news when it challenged the seating of an all-white delegation at the 1964 Democratic Convention. Between 1965 and 1969 black registration in Mississippi had increased from 28,000 to more than 260,000. By 1969

5. Ibid.

this registration had resulted in Negroes being elected to 89 public and party offices in Mississippi.[6] One of these offices was that of state senator and another was mayor of Fayette. In itself these statistics are not very significant but prior to the nonviolent campaigns in the South, Mississippi had no black elected officials.

Meanwhile CORE, under the leadership of James Farmer, in 1961 organized the famous Freedom Rides to Alabama and Mississippi to put an end to segregated public transportation. A bus was burned, freedom riders were beaten, and many of them served time in Mississippi prisons. But the nonviolent action caused the Interstate Commerce Commission to issue an order desegregating all interstate transportation. By 1963 the action moved into northern cities with the cry of "Freedom Now." Street demonstrations and some boycotts compelled "employers, from supermarkets to banks, to add many Negroes to their work force in Northern and Western cities, in some Southern cities, and even in some Southern towns where the Negroes had considerable buying power."[7]

The March on Washington in August 1963, in which about a quarter of a million people participated, about twenty percent of whom were white, led to the passage of the Civil Rights Act of 1964 which opened places of public accommodation for Negroes. The next step was the Voting Rights Act of 1965 on the heels of the demonstration at Selma, Alabama, led by Martin Luther King and the Southern Christian Leadership Conference.

The series of nonviolent actions was interrupted by spontaneous explosions or racial rebellions in cities across the country. Some have suggested that the riots produced concessions in Congress and in northern cities. There is no hard evidence to support this. The various riots or racial disturbances in cities across the country have been under-

6. *Washington* (D.C.) *Sunday Star*, 30 November 1969.
7. *Report of National Advisory Commission*, p. 231.

stood as spontaneous explosions. For the most part they have neither been rewarded by important white concessions nor penalized by serious retribution. The chief institutionalized results of the riots are plans by police and army units for more effective containment of the ghetto. Military planning institutions like RAND and the Institute for Defense Analysis engaged in planning for urban warfare. The Army Operation Center on the second floor of the Pentagon became a national command post for troops engaged in urban control. There are comprehensive plans for every city, including exact location of all critical installations that must be protected, areas for troop concentrations, etc. In New York City a "war room" was established at 51 Chambers Street staffed by eight experts.[8]

Representative Richard Bolling asserted in May 1968:

The rioting in Washington, D.C. and elsewhere did *not* cause Congress to pass this [open housing] legislation. The record is clear on this point and I cannot emphasize it too strongly. Violence did not bring about the Federal open-housing law, as some black militants and their white supporters assert. Equally false is the allegation by white segregationists that the Congress was "stampeded" or "panicked" into passage by the violence. The undeniable truth is that the Senate had already passed the fair housing legislation on March 11, weeks before the disturbances broke out in many cities beginning April 4, the day Dr. King was murdered. Correspondingly the House had begun action long before the rioting erupted. In March the House Rules Committee formally voted to take its final action on the open housing bill on April 9, and the House leadership expected to bring the bill to the floor the next day.[9]

Everything went according to this schedule and the House passed it.

The accomplishments of a series of nonviolent actions can be summarized as follows: the desegregation of places

8. *New York Post*, 13 April 1968, *Vietnam Report*, Summer 1968, p. 43.
9. Richard Bolling, "Report From Washington," May 1968.

of public accommodation in more than a dozen northern cities and then nationally, the desegregation of the armed forces, the ending of racial discrimination in public transportation, the inclusion of black delegates in southern state delegations to national political conventions, the Voting Rights Act of 1965, the widespread practice of business and educational establishments employing some black people in other than menial jobs, the Open Housing Act of 1968, and various local, political and economic gains.

One of the major achievements of the nonviolent actions was the focusing of national attention by both black and white persons on the racial crisis. This in turn led many stores and industries to begin employment of black people, not to stave off armed violence, but to prevent selective boycott. In the long run probably the most important result of the nonviolent movement was to give black people a sense of dignity and achievement. They could, even in the South, accomplish some political change; they did have power when they organized against a system, and they did command respect because thousands of whites joined their campaign while accepting their leadership. The "black is beautiful" slogan is simply one more manifestation of that new-found dignity and of the need to expand it and make it permanent.

Unfortunately nonviolent direct action did not bring a complete change in black-white relations. Nor did it eliminate de facto school segregation, inferior schools, police brutality, slum housing, unemployment, and underemployment. Millions of whites assumed that the passage of the Civil Rights Act of 1964 and the Voting Rights Act of 1965 had brought real gains for black Americans. These whites saw Negroes gaining access to the same hotels, restaurants, and places of entertainment that they enjoyed, but they did not stop to think that the great majority of blacks are either too poor to eat in restaurants or stay in hotels, or that, when they do leave the black ghetto, an unsegregated facility is only a drop in an empty bucket.

The impact of the Voting Rights Act was described by Martin Luther King as follows:

What was minimally required in the law was the appointment of hundreds of registrars and thousands of Federal marshals to inhibit Southern terror. Instead, fewer than forty registrars were appointed and not a single Federal law officer capable of making an arrest was sent into the South. As a consequence the old way of life—economic coercion, terrorism, murder and inhuman contempt—continued unabated.

The usual criticism of nonviolence by some blacks can be summarized as follows: (1) it did not function fast enough; (2) it did not solve the problems of the black poor; and (3) it did not develop an effective strategy for northern cities, but was largely a Southern strategy.

In general these criticisms are correct, but this is because of the deep-rooted racism in our society, rather than because violence is a better method. The Black Panthers, for example, have not produced any gains commensurate with those of Martin Luther King even though they have been in existence much longer than the two-year period of the Montgomery bus boycott. The bodyguards of the Black Panther party leaders have been less effective in preventing the death of their leaders than have nonviolent groups who function without bodyguards. Not a single Panther has been saved from death by a bodyguard. Instead they have tended to provoke violence and violent reaction. Some Panthers have already been killed and others have fled the country. David McReynolds wrote in the January 1970 *W.R.L. News*, that if the Panthers "are to survive [they] must turn to unarmed whites for help," which means that "the logic of nonviolence applies not only to the South, but to the North as well." McReynolds also observed that "the remaining Panthers are riddled with mutual suspicion because they are riddled with police agents, something which is going to happen to any group in this country which seeks victory through a secret conspiracy rather than an open revolution."

However, by the middle of the 1960s, militant black members of SNCC, CORE, and other groups began to believe that the real problems facing black people had not been and would not be solved by nonviolent means. "At the very time that white support for the protest movement was rising markedly," said the National Advisory Commission on Civil Disorders, militant Negroes began to talk of "retaliatory violence, and increasingly rejected white assistance. They insisted that Negro power alone could compel the white 'ruling class' to make concessions."[10]

The war in Vietnam began to divert the attention of many white liberals, while the riots of 1967 and the violent rhetoric of some black militants alienated still others. Instead of building on the nonviolent successes to go on to other campaigns and instead of continued cooperation with those whites who were gradually becoming radicalized, many militant blacks began to talk of guerrilla warfare and to believe that whites would only respond when there was a base of black power capable of intimidating the white power structure. The result was a series of "black manifestoes" demanding money from white churches, a series of demands that flowed from black caucuses set up in almost all racially mixed organizations, and in some cities, direct confrontations with the police.

The major psychological achievement of the nonviolent action and the impressive leadership of Martin Luther King and his colleagues was to create in white liberals a great feeling of guilt, which was prerequisite to their willingness to change the system that had for so long been built on white vested interests. But this guilt needed time if it was to be translated into significant concrete political action that would be really liberating. Black militants were unwilling to take time because they saw "time" as equivalent to the gradualism of earlier years which was an excuse

10. *Report of National Advisory Commission*, pp. 231–32.

to do nothing. At the very point when the white mood was capable of being changed, the trend toward violent rhetoric and the glorification of black violence tended to eliminate or sublimate the guilt of many whites and thus permit a kind of false righteousness or self-righteousness. This was expressed in various ways: "Black racism is as bad as white racism," or "We cannot risk the general white backlash by appearing to defend a violent black movement," or "I am still for racial equality but I can't go along with violence." As a result white contributions to CORE and SNCC, which had abandoned their former policies of nonviolence, dried up, and even the Southern Christian Leadership Conference which remained nonviolent began to feel the financial pinch.

Most whites simply did not understand that the black rhetoric of violence was a psychological necessity for some blacks. They had to express their manhood in the same way that many white males have expressed theirs. This was especially true when they realized that they could not sustain the momentum of the early campaigns. Some believe that the rhetoric of black violence was a result of the decline in financial support, membership, and activity of CORE and SNCC and therefore a product of frustration and impotence. If this is the case the rhetoric of violence simply accelerated the decline and led to further frustration. The report of the National Advisory Commission on Civil Disorders contains a significant and accurate analysis of the rhetoric of violence:

Black power rhetoric and ideology actually express a lack of power. . . . Powerless to make any fundamental changes in the life of the masses—powerless, that is, to compel white America to make those changes—many advocates of Black Power have retreated into an unreal world, where they see an outnumbered and poverty-stricken minority organizing itself independently of whites and creating sufficient power to force white America to grant its demands. To date the evidence suggests that the situation is much like that of the 1840's, when a small group of intellectuals advocated slave insurrections, but stopped short of organizing them.

The Black Power advocates of today consciously feel that they are the most militant group in the Negro protest movement. Yet they have retreated from a direct confrontation with American society on the issue of integration and, by preaching separatism, unconsciously function as an accommodation to white racism. Much of their economic program, as well as their interest in Negro history, self-help, racial solidarity and separation is reminiscent of Booker T. Washington. The rhetoric is different, but the programs are remarkably similar.[11]

Whites must face the fact that black separatism, however mistaken, is a reaction to white racism. Most whites thought that the goal of blacks was integration. Whites, however, defined integration as the assimilation of blacks into the white community and its churches, schools, clubs, etc., preferably on a basis proportional to the general population so that whites would not be outnumbered. Black people, on the other hand, were not interested in assimilation or becoming white, but believed that integration was a two-way street. Why should whites not become a part of a predominantly black neighborhood, school, church, etc., if they are prepared to abandon racism? It is the rejection of the white concept of integration that led to the idea of black separatism. Instead of debating the merits of integration which now has too many emotional overtones, it is better to seek liberation. In the racial context liberation means that blacks are completely free either to associate among themselves without having whites present or to have whites present. Liberation means that blacks and whites must be inwardly free to live and move entirely, chiefly, or occasionally with those who by race or color are different. This necessarily means the end of all politically, socially, or economically enforced segregation and discrimination.

For some blacks, separatism is liberation because they

11. Ibid., pp. 234–35.

believe they will get away from white control. Liberation however is not achieved by living in a separate state or going back to Africa or maintaining tight ghettos controlled by blacks. This idea of separatism is based on a colonial analysis—that black people are an internal colony quite as much as India or Algeria were colonies. The assumption that if they can take control over a particular part of a city or of an entire state they will achieve freedom is akin to the idea of getting rid of a colonial power. There is some truth to this, and some validity to the idea of black leadership and control of an all-black school or ghetto, if they have to be all-black. But colonies that have achieved a certain political independence are not thereby economically free. Most former colonies have to exist within the economic orbit of the United States, Western Europe, or the Soviet Union. They are, in other words, "underdeveloped" and therefore in a different economic class or situation than the ruling nations. A black-controlled state or numerous black-controlled ghettos are not thereby economically free. Liberation therefore must include economic power, because politically independent groups that are economically dependent are always at the mercy of those who control the supply of food, raw materials, industrial products and finance. In a liberated society there will be both black and white executives, managers, and foremen who are in those positions because of ability rather than color. However, the ability of every black or white child now living in poverty cannot be made fully available to the community without an adequate family income and good schools. This suggests many solutions, such as expanded black registration and voting to achieve political power, guaranteed annual incomes of at least $6,ooo per family, black banks, Project Equality to encourage black business, black cooperatives, and various other forms of economic power as steps toward liberation. All of these assume a continuation of either a capitalist or a mixed economy. Some blacks, however, as well as some whites, doubt the ability of our society to achieve any important degree of liberation without transforming it into a democratic socialist society. This cannot be done by the black community alone, and still less by a few cadres of black militants alone.

On the other hand, it is extremely difficult if not impossible for white men to be the liberators of black men. They do not share the same experiences or feel the same day-after-day indignities and suffering. Hence, they do not have the same incentive to become involved in a liberation movement. Most whites who engaged in the civil rights campaigns were only occasional or part-time participants. Most of them did not cut themselves off from their families or their work. They returned to their schools or jobs after the demonstrations were over. In the new situation, even nonviolent black movements are not seeking part-time white participation, but look to whites chiefly for financial and legal assistance.

A second reason for the inability of white men to be liberators is their part in the structures of society that keep black men "in their place." They may be just, friendly and open in their personal relationships with black persons but they do not participate in the process of liberation unless they seek actively to eliminate or drastically to change the structures that keep men bound. No great price is required in our society today to establish a personal relationship between black and white persons of the same economic and educational status. Such relationships if kept on the occasional intellectual or discussion basis became relatively common in the late fifties and sixties. But a price is more likely to be required of any man who makes fundamental attacks on the political, economic, military, religious, and social institutions which sustain the power structures of our society. Institutions, as the name implies, "institutionalize" or stabilize the values of society. They tend to be bastions of the status quo rather than agents for its destruction or transformation. Few churches, white political organizations, or economic associations ever concern themselves with the laws broken by white men who do violence to black men, but these same groups are vigorous about maintaining law and order in the face of riots, looting and even quiet pilfering by black people. Martin Luther King in 1967 explained this double standard:

It is incontestable and deplorable that Negroes have committed crimes, but they are derivative crimes. They are born of the greater crimes of the white society. When we ask Negroes to abide by the law, let us also declare that the white man does not abide by laws of the ghettos. Day in and day out he violates welfare laws to deprive the poor of their meager allotments; he flagrantly violates building codes and regulations; his police make a mockery of law; he violates laws on equal employment and education and the provisions for civic services. The slums are the handiwork of a vicious system of the white society; Negroes live in them, but they do not make them, any more than a prisoner makes a prison.[12]

Sometimes white men argue that they are not a part of institutions that hold black men down, just as many Germans during the Hitler period professed not to know what was happening to Jews in Germany. The problem is not simply one of being involved in the planning or preserving of unfreedom, but is chiefly one of acquiescing in it, of failing to join in liberating activity. From the standpoint of redemptive ethics, white men should acknowledge the worth and importance of black rebellion. In such a rebellion the main task of repentant white men is to rid our own house of the things which have caused the rebellion. These include attitudes and structures. Glen Trimble has suggested:

We must first recognize the division of labor in our society which allows us to be both comfortable and nonviolent because we have built an elaborate legal structure and assigned, financed,

12. Martin Luther King, Jr., *The Trumpet of Conscience* (New York: Harper and Row, 1967), p. 8.

and armed to the teeth special forces to be violent on our be-
half.

If then we cannot bring ourselves to challenge and repudiate
this entire arrangement we can at least assume the responsibilities that are still ours—to police the police, to defend the defenseless, to restructure law to bring human rights somewhere
nearer property rights, to drastically reduce *both* official and
unofficial armament.[13]

Some white men will go beyond these suggestions to
challenge and confront specific power structures whose
very existence perpetuates racial oppression. But if liberation is to come it will be "black and white together" on
black initiative. Martin Luther King, before his death,
pointed to a new strategy for the North. He said:

The effectiveness of street marches in cities is limited because
the normal turbulence of city life absorbs them as mere transi-
tory drama quite common to the ordinary movement of masses.
In the South, a march was a social earthquake; in the North, it
is a faint, brief exclamation of protest.[14]

King believed there had to be a strategy that corre-
sponded to "heightened black impatience and stiffened
white resistance." That strategy would have to involve
"mass civil disobedience." The demonstrations or marches
in effect were "a statement to the larger society. . . ." Now
there had to be something more, "a force that interrupts its
functioning at some key point." But "that interruption
must not . . . be clandestine. . . . It must be open and,
above all conducted by large masses without violence." The
imprisonment of many blacks, he felt, would help the
cause. In effect the Negro would be saying: "I am not
avoiding penalties for breaking the law—I am willing to
endure all your punishment because your society will not

13. Glen Trimble, from an informal memorandum prepared
for the National Council of Churches, Crisis in the Nation
Program, New York, 1969.
14. King, *Conscience*, p. 14.

be able to endure the stigma of violently and publicly oppressing its minority to preserve injustice."

Without disclosing exactly what he had in mind, King talked about dislocating the functioning of a city so that it would be costly without being destructive. He held that violence "is not revolutionary but reactionary, because it invites defeat. It involves an emotional catharsis, but it must be followed by a sense of futility."[15]

King also talked about selective boycotts, possibly building on the experience with the bus boycott in Montgomery. A Chicano leader, Cesar Chavez, demonstrated the value of a selective boycott in combination with a strike. The strategy of boycott has also been successfully used to secure jobs for blacks in various companies in Chicago in "Operation Breadbasket," led by Jesse Jackson.

How do the powerless come into control of their own destiny? There is no single strategy that will always work. But the lessons learned since 1940 are these: Organized demonstrations by black people were necessary to the building of black confidence and solidarity. They were also necessary as a device to tell whites the truth about segregation and white racism. Boycotts, sit-ins, strikes, and other forms of black power achieved the specific goals sought but fell short of complete equality and freedom. Impatience and frustration with nonviolent methods and leadership led to the use by black militants of violence and the rhetoric of violence. These frightened many blacks as well as the great majority of whites, with the result that few if any gains can be traced to threats or actual violence. However, the cumulative impact of the militant nonviolence and the rhetoric of black power has created a sense of determination and dignity that are prerequisite to future struggle.

15. Ibid., p. 15.

12

CONCLUSION

LIBERATION BEGINS with a consciousness of oppression which has developed within a community that is trapped by one or more systems of violence. These systems, as Marx indicated, operate in the interests of a dominant group or class. They are not, however, identical with the groups that benefit from them. It is the relationship any group has with the system that determines whether it is oppressor or oppressed. Liberation ethics builds on this idea to indicate that supporters of an oppressive system are adversaries only because of their relation to the system, and will cease to be adversaries under new social structures. It recognizes that most oppressive structures are the product of many generations and many persons. They are not dependent on the survival of a particular group of persons but have a semiindependent existence because of their wide acceptance by the general population, or because of the alleged benefits they bring to society, or because they are imbedded in or related to other structures deemed valuable to society.

Gandhi demonstrated that any powerful group of men such as those who administer a system in their own interest are powerful only as the masses of people obey them or cooperate with them. The power of the few can be withdrawn by the noncooperation of the many. Both Gandhi and King held that it is possible to distinguish between the system and the supporters of the system. Those who support the system are to be respected as fellow human beings while the system is being eliminated or transformed.

The emphasis on systems as the major source of oppression does not, however, mean that systems have no relation to men. Neither does it mean that liberation ethics can or does neglect the transformation of persons. As has already been suggested, there is a direct relationship between the action men use to seize power and the way they exercise it; a connection between the kind of persons who participate in revolution and the consequences of revolutionary action.

Liberation ethics' view of man is a combination of the Christian view that man is alienated from God and his fellow men and the Marxist view that there is a gap or chasm between what man is and his potential. Marx saw the system in which man lived as contributing to his alienation because a worker could not fulfill himself in his work. "The laborer exists for the process of production and not the process of production for the laborer."[1] The Christian concept of alienation is that man is at enmity with God because of his enmity with his fellow men. This enmity is rooted in each man's tendency to place his own security and interests ahead of the security and well-being of his fellow men. The enmity is expressed in fear, hatred, anger, guilt, greed, and other enslaving emotions. If men and women are to be truly liberated, they must transform the systems that contribute to their alienation as capitalism does with its production for the profit of the few at the expense of the many and as war does by institutionalizing different national groupings into armed rivalry.

True liberation also involves freedom from enmity. That freedom comes as a result of repentance and reconciliation. Repentance is an acknowledgement of implication in enmity and a decision to be united with rather than alienated from one's fellows. It begins with the assumption that

1. Karl Marx, *Capital* (Chicago: Charles H. Kerr and Company, 1906), p. 536.

the changing of a system or the changing of an adversary begins with change of oneself. It means that I have no control over the president of any corporation or of the corporate financial system nor over the president or dictator of any nation. The only person over whom I have any control is myself. Therefore if I want to change the system or the nation or the world I must start at the point where I have some control. If I condone the system instead of withdrawing support from it, there is no evident repentance for my share in the oppression or exploitation caused by the system.

Reconciliation is the process of turning enemies into friends. Traditional revolutionary thinking does not offer real hope of liberation because it has no doctrine of reconciliation with enemies; their only choice is submission or extinction. Those who support the violent seizure of power or civil war may have a doctrine of postponed reconciliation. The basic difference between those who choose nonviolent methods and those who choose violent action under certain conditions can be summarized by saying that both believe in ending injustice and oppression, whereas the former believes reconciliation must be implicit in their action against oppression while the latter believes reconciliation must be sought after the shooting and the bombing end, with those who are still alive.

Some white extremists and black militants define reconciliation in such a way as to make it meaningless. They say that reconciliation is the process whereby persons who have been alienated from each other are restored to unity or harmony. However, they also say that since the races have always been separated, it is impossible to bring together again those who were never at any time together. Reconciliation, however, is not simply a reuniting of people who were at one time united and have since become estranged. It is the uniting of persons who are divided for whatever reason but who belong together because of their common humanity. Reconciliation in its broadest sense means that there is a fundamental human unity which is deeper than any physical, religious, national, or ideological difference.

The ideas of personal responsibility for changing the structures of society implicit in the concept of repentance and of group struggle to achieve the transformation of oppressing systems are combined with reconciliation in the methods and strategies of nonviolent direct action. The emphasis on nonviolence is not on the mere absence of violence, but on a method of social struggle derived from the models set forth by Jesus, Gandhi, King, and others. The fact that persons are nonviolent is no guarantee of safety. Their persistent attack on structured or systemic violence is likely to produce a strong reaction from those who identify with the system under attack. Suffering is therefore always the price of liberation. The cross in Christian symbolism expresses the reality of costliness involved in seeking the liberation of men from any powerful enslaving interest. Liberation in Christian as well as in Gandhian thought is costly in a special way. It is understood as requiring the paying of a price oneself, instead of exacting it from others. It implies that liberation is not accomplished by freeing one group of people by enslaving or destroying another.

The outlining of concepts such as repentance, reconciliation, nonviolent struggle, and the willingness to suffer, clearly indicates that moral men and women are necessary participants in the process of liberation. A moral man is one who strives intensely to let nothing stand in the way of liberation. He is a new person, not only because of his commitment to liberation of all persons but also because he is involved in the struggle now. He is disciplined so as to avoid the initial steps that may lead to addictive habits or to the acceptance of comfort or anything else that might stand in the way of pursuing his goal. The moral man views liberation both as the product of transformed systems and as a process in which he is expressing his respect for other persons. He is aware that the test of liberation is not simply in loyalty to it as a goal but in the consequences achieved. He has a duty to consider and foresee the various possible consequences of his action. But this is extremely difficult and perhaps impossible in complex situations. Therefore the means or methods are emphasized as the basis for action.

As Berdyaev pointed out:

> There is a great mystery concealed in the fact that the means are more important than the end. It is precisely the means they employ, the way they take, which bears witness to the spirit by which people are imbued. . . . The future in which the exalted end was to be realized never comes. In it there will again be those same repulsive means. Violence never leads to freedom. Hatred never leads to brotherhood.[2]

The moral man, in other words, is not moved chiefly by anger or rage at those who administer the system, but plans his strategy carefully.

Some proponents of armed revolution, however, would contend that by nature, revolution is not a rational approach to change. It comes only when there is bitterness about oppression or a breaking of relationships between the ruling class and those intellectuals and others who are a bridge to the poor or outcast. They would insist that revolutions "break out" rather than occur as a result of careful planning. History reveals that some revolutions are more or less spontaneous or the result of events that were not intended to lead to violence. The French Revolution is an illustration of this type. But the Chinese, Algerian, and Cuban revolutions were planned by rational men who were accustomed to think of power in terms of violence. In the modern world those who seriously contemplate liberation cannot afford the luxury of unplanned or spontaneous yielding to hatred or vengeance and violence. They have before them enough evidence about nonviolent forms of

2. Nicholas Berdyaev, *Slavery and Freedom* (London: Geoffrey Bles, The Centenary Press, 1943), p. 195.

power that they need not repeat the mistakes of their ancestors.

"Unlike the violent strategist," wrote Martin Oppenheimer,

the non-violent practitioner sees means and ends, the present and the future, as being dialectically interrelated. The means he uses are themselves revolutionary; thereby they create a qualitatively different end than that of the reformer who uses present-day bourgeois (corrupt) means or the violent revolutionary who at some point must cut himself off completely from legal means and work for a cataclysmic change in the future. Only in the non-violent revolutionary movement can a participant behave both "civilly" and subversively at the same time, hence the term "creative disorder" as opposed to the destructive disorder which is the pre-requisite for a takeover by a violent revolutionary group.[3]

Much opposition to revolutionary movements comes from assumptions that they are not concerned with means. They have failed to provide people either with a vision of the society they want or with an understanding of how they hope to achieve it. They have created an image for most Americans that if they have their way we shall be in for a long period of havoc or disorder. In part this image stems from some mass protests in Washington, New York, Chicago, and Berkeley which have had biased newspaper coverage across the country. In large part it comes from the rhetoric of violence. But the image also comes from actual bombings and other violent activity which the bulk of the American people are not likely to accept. Groups that are prepared to use any means tend to communicate this to people. Their image of being unprincipled increases resistance to their program and makes it less likely that they will gain the support they want.

A lack of concern for means is evident in the language some groups use in their dismissal of potential sympa-

3. Martin Oppenheimer, *The Urban Guerrilla* (Chicago: Quadrangle Books, 1969), p. 130.

thizers. By calling whole groups of people "racists" or
"pigs" or "hard hats" or "straights" or "establishment liberals," they indicate that these people are hopeless. A
group genuinely concerned with liberation will not cut itself off from any segment of the community by developing
a rhetoric or jargon that automatically marks some people
as irrevocable adversaries, whether these are police, soldiers, or other administrators, or defenders of an oppressive system. Ultimately there is no chance of making any
system illegitimate if those now supporting such systems
are, by permanent hostility, precluded from withdrawing
their support. Instead of such enmity, a strategy of liberation will include efforts to establish personal relationships
with natural adversaries. These personal contacts must be
based on genuine respect and understanding but designed
to encourage and challenge such adversaries to live up to
their own convictions and highest expectations. In the case
of police this would mean at least a respect for minorities,
a devotion to civil liberties for everyone, and a recognition
of the need for changing rather than supporting unjust
systems. The war in Vietnam demonstrated that many soldiers, veterans, and others who were "hopelessly" prowar
could be and were in fact won to the antiwar cause. Respect for personality and the demonstration of a humanizing concern for people "after the revolution" must begin
before the major revolutionary events if they are to be
credible. There is a pragmatic as well as a religious aspect
to choosing appropriate means for liberation. The millions
of people who daily experience hardship, injustice, or some
other form of oppression are not likely to follow blindly
those whose seizure of power may create more oppression.
Many of them have a job or a mortgaged house or some
modest investment that ties them to existing political and
economic systems. They need to understand that revolution
will increase rather than damage the little bit of security
they have. The exemplification of a concern for means
improves the chances of success of any revolutionary

group. The religious aspect about means is that they are determined by respect for all persons without regard to their potential usefulness to the revolutionary goal. The moral man is one whose respect for persons is a matter of conviction, however much he may recognize the usefulness of nonviolent means to his cause.

Most people have difficulty understanding how a revolution can be other than dehumanizing or violent. They believe that all revolutionaries want to get control of the nation by violent means. They fear such control of state power will be used to oppress rather than liberate. If, on the other hand, radical social change begins in local communities and without violence, these fears are seriously undercut. It is also more possible to begin locally to demonstrate a new quality of life. Anyone who wants to change the world must, as already noted, begin with the person over whom he has the most control: himself. He must take personal responsibility for the existing violence, to eliminate it within himself, and to begin to expand his influence to others. If it is impossible to persuade fellow students or fellow workers or others with whom there is some sympathetic tie, it may be difficult to begin elsewhere.

It is essential to organize groups dedicated to radical social change. Those groups must engage in serious study or research about local and national structures as a background for political and economic analysis. They must develop a common or united approach to social change based on the life style of Jesus or Gandhi or some contemporary strategy of liberation rooted in respect for persons. Their approach to social change is determined ethically by the goals they seek, their motivation in seeking it, the method or means they use to achieve it, and the consequences or probable consequences of their action. All of these criteria are conditioned by and help determine the group's political analysis that is prerequisite to action. Such political analysis (including economic and sociological factors) involves the following: (1) an understanding of the historical roots of contemporary problems and prior approaches toward solving similar problems; (2) a wide reading of a spectrum of political interpretations of the contemporary scene; (3) listening to the dissenters and the oppressed in our society and involving them in meaningful dialogue; and (4) evaluating, in searching discussions within the basic committed community, the tentative political conclusions with their ethical, theological, and ideological assumptions before coming to an action decision.

Political analysis overlaps with strategizing as to the courses of action to pursue. Implicit in the planning of strategy are numerous considerations such as the following: How to focus on the systemic problems rather than simply on a few individuals connected with the system; what are the values and disvalues of the system; what are the vulnerable points of the system; how can they be exposed and at what points is noncooperation feasible; and are there biblical, historical, or contemporary models for liberation that reveal insight or ways of dealing with oppressive structures.

Any group that seriously intends social change must oppose the structures of violence in its own vicinity. In doing so the chief needs are for research so that all available facts about the structure are known; for imagination in attacking them or in creating alternate structures; and organization of the poor, or segregated, the students, consumers, workers, or some other power base. Those who are organized should share a common need for liberation so that they participate in action to achieve realizable goals while learning the methods of more far-reaching change.

It is significant that the nationwide civil rights campaign began not with a meeting of nationally known leaders, but in Montgomery, Alabama, with black ministers Martin Luther King, Ralph Abernathy, and others who were not known outside of their own city. It was the successful bus boycott with its superior organization, discipline, and leadership that made possible the sit-ins and other campaigns throughout the nation. The challenge of structures of violence can be as effective on the local level as on any other. Their effectiveness will not only transform local structures but also serve as regional or national models.

Groups organized for social change locally must avoid being caught up in national political campaigns as if these campaigns are all-important, or more significant than community action. It is very easy to mislead the American people as Woodrow Wilson, Franklin Roosevelt, and Lyndon Johnson did with their campaign promises to keep the United States out of direct involvement in war. The American political system has certain strengths but it is designed to prevent rather than facilitate transformation of the basic structures of our society such as monopoly capitalism or the tax structures that provide loopholes for the rich and heavy penalties for middle- and lower-income groups. The great American deception is the public-relations impression that the two major political parties offer alternative courses of action. The minor differences between parties or between regional and other interests are used to create the impression of democracy while the basic systems are strengthened in the interest of a few hundred corporations and a few thousand individuals. Liberation as such is never an issue. Even minor differences revealed in congressional debate are adjusted by compromises that often deflect attention away from the real issues. These compromises are rationalized with such slogans as "politics is the art of the possible" or "politics is the art of compromise." The result is that many Americans are seduced into accepting what they do not want. The fact of a two-party system and the virtual ignoring of minority parties led many students to assert in the 1960s that "voting is a passive act, a choosing between alternatives provided by someone else."[4] Those students became convinced from the civil rights campaign and the Vietnam war that voting, even when a majority of the people

4. Steve Halliwell, "Personal Liberation and Social Change," *New Left Notes*, 4 September 1967, p. 1.

were opposed to the Vietnam war or to restrictions on blacks in southern political life, did not solve these problems.

It is the unfortunate failing of the American political system that it is impossible to vote for or against issues or political philosophies. Instead, voting is for or against individual candidates who cannot be held to their election promises. This led the Methodist board of Christian Social Concerns in February 1968 to adopt a statement which said: "Any analysis which fails to note the value of non-voting or a protest vote for a given office does not adequately face the electoral problem. A vote may be thrown away on a candidate who does not tolerably represent one's political convictions quite as much as by failing to vote."

Given the problems of electoral politics, some Americans committed to social change have decided to try to gain control of a major party by organizing at the grass-roots level to control the choice of those who go to the presidential nominating conventions. To control the major party in this way would involve a national organization with some access to money and media coverage that those devoted to radical social change might find difficult to get. While this should not be ruled out, a sounder approach is to recognize that election campaigns in the United States are not likely to deal with the fundamental issues or produce basic structural changes.

Martin Luther King said in this context:

I have come to think of my role as one which operates outside the realm of partisan politics, raising the issues and through action creating the situation which forces whatever party is in power to act creatively in response to the dramatic presentation of these issues on the public scene.[5]

This means that those who seek liberation can build local organizations that will confront and change the decisions of urban developers, loan sharks, chain stores, the police, boards of education, and other groups away from

5. *New York Times*, 26 April 1967.

discrimination against the poor and minorities. Project Equality is an illustration of healthy though moderate and nonrevolutionary local confrontation. It seeks to get corporations, stores, churches, and other institutions that purchase services or goods, to buy only from those who hire persons without regard to race. In a large midwestern city, one chain store has met Project Equality requirements. A local group, in buying food products only from that chain store, periodically sends all receipts from the checkout counter to the management of another chain store it is seeking to influence.

Operation Breadbasket of Chicago and greater New York has led demonstrations, sit-ins, and boycotts against bakeries and supermarket chains. On October 6, 1971, a corporation which has 168 supermarkets in the New York area agreed to fill "up to 20 per cent" of its jobs with blacks and other minority members, even though blacks accounted for only about seven percent of the chain's business. In addition the chain agreed to an identical goal for deposits in black-owned banks and expenditures on black-owned advertising, insurance, and service businesses.[6]

These represent positive ways of boycotting. Other actions may be more revolutionary or involve greater risks. The haunting of public officials, business leaders or other citizens is a more dramatic course of action. If a few hundred black and white persons backed by reserves of one or two thousand others (in case of arrest), were daily to appear in small groups at the homes and offices of public officials, always with some symbol of their oppression and always with a specific goal such as municipal ownership of the local gas or electric utility, it would create an immediate community debate. It would need to be backed with adequate research to demonstrate that the profits saved would result in lower rates; and with informed persons who present their case in various ways to the people of the community.

6. *New York Times*, 7 October 1971.

This is not the place to outline a program for community action. Such action cannot be blueprinted but must arise out of the needs of those who feel in their bodies or minds that they have had all the injustice they are prepared to take and now want to do something about it. This is, however, the place to indicate that revolutions ought always to grow out of human need and ought always to transform systems rather than destroy persons.

The fundamental difference between liberation and political liberalism is that the former seeks to eliminate or transform systems and structures of violence, whereas the latter seeks to maintain the basic structures while trying to improve them gradually. The fundamental differences between liberation ethics and a traditional revolutionary approach are that the former believes a humanizing result requires nonviolent means and can usually be achieved best through a progressive conquest of power, whereas the latter emphasizes the use of violence, usually with the aim of a military or paramilitary seizure of the central government.

Liberation ethics also views the struggle against oppression as a continuing one. There is no final revolution which by definition brings utopia. It is possible to end specific systems such as human slavery, monopoly capitalism, war, subordination of women, and racial segregation; but the ending and replacement of such systems is simply a crucial part of a much longer task of continuing liberation. That task belongs to everybody but uniquely to those who are committed to human freedom. There is such a thing as the liberation of a person's intelligence and will so that he or she is prepared to live as if the liberated community were already here. Such persons will associate with each other to begin the process of structural change and the liberation of others. Anyone who behaves on a lower level of freedom than he can, diminishes and helps destroy freedom for others. Something extraordinary is required of those who want to be free and who want others to be free.

Index